SCIENCE
In Your World

SENIOR AUTHORS

Dr. Jay K. Hackett
Dr. Richard H. Moyer

Macmillan/McGraw-Hill
School Publishing Company

ACKNOWLEDGMENTS

For permission to reprint copyrighted material, grateful acknowledgment is made to the following authors, publishers, and agents. All possible care has been taken to trace the ownership of every selection included and to make full acknowledgment of its use. If any errors have inadvertently occurred, they will be corrected in subsequent editions, provided notification is sent to the publisher.

Jonathan Cape Ltd.: From *The Poetry of Robert Frost* edited by Edward Connery Lathem. Copyright 1928, 1939, © 1967, 1969 by Holt, Rinehart and Winston. Copyright © 1956 by Robert Frost. Reprinted by permission of Robert Frost, the editor.

Eleanor Farjeon: Text excerpt from "Bedtime" from *Eleanor Farjeon's Poems for Children* by Eleanor Farjeon. Reprinted by permission of David Higham Associates, Ltd.

Harper & Row, Publishers, Inc.: Text excerpt from "Bedtime" from *Eleanor Farjeon's Poems for Children* by Eleanor Farjeon.

Lippincott: "Bedtime" originally appeared in *Over the Garden Wall* by Eleanor Farjeon. Copyright 1933, renewed 1961 by Eleanor Farjeon.

Harold Ober Associates, Incorporated: From "Bedtime" from *Over the Garden Wall*, reprinted by permission of Harold Ober Associates Incorporated, copyright © 1933, 1961 by Eleanor Farjeon.

Henry Holt and Company, Inc.: From "Keepsakes" from *Is Somewhere Always Far Away?* by Leland B. Jacobs, copyright © 1967 by Leland B. Jacobs. Reprinted by permission of Henry Holt and Company, Inc. "Lodged" from *The Poetry of Robert Frost,* edited by Edward Connery Lathem. Copyright 1928, 1939, © 1967, 1969 by Holt, Rinehart and Winston. Copyright © 1956 by Robert Frost. Reprinted by permission of Henry Holt and Company, Inc.

CREDITS

Series Editor: Jane Parker
Design Coordinator: Kip Frankenberry
Series Production Editor: Helen Mischka
Level Editors: Patricia Morooka-Barr, Patricia A. Evans
Contributing Editors: Barbara A. Everett, Beverlee Jobrack
Production Editor: Jillian C. Yerkey
Designer: Brent Good
Artist: Lynda Kae Harper
Photo Editor: Mark Burnett

Macmillan/McGraw-Hill School Division
866 Third Avenue
New York, New York 10022

Printed in the United States of America

ISBN 0-675-16227-0

9 8 7 6 5 4 3

SENIOR AUTHORS

Dr. Jay K. Hackett
University of Northern Colorado

Dr. Richard H. Moyer
University of Michigan-Dearborn

CONTRIBUTING AUTHORS

Stephen C. Blume
Elementary Science Curriculum Specialist
St. Tammany Public School System
Slidell, Louisiana

Ralph M. Feather, Jr.
Teacher of Geology, Astronomy, and Earth Science
Derry Area School District
Derry, Pennsylvania

Edward Paul Ortleb
Science Supervisor
St. Louis Board of Education
St. Louis, Missouri

Dr. Barbara Swanson Thomson
Associate Professor in Science Education
The Ohio State University
Columbus, Ohio

CONTRIBUTING WRITER
Ann H. Sankey
Science Specialist
Educational Service District 121
Seattle, Washington

READING CONSULTANT
Barbara S. Pettegrew, Ph.D.
Director of the Reading/Study Center
Assistant Professor of Education
Otterbein College, Westerville, Ohio

SAFETY CONSULTANT
Gary E. Downs, Ed.D.
Professor
Iowa State University
Ames, Iowa

GIFTED AND MAINSTREAMED CONSULTANTS

George Fichter
Educational Consultant
Programs for Gifted
Ohio Department of Education
Worthington, Ohio

Timothy E. Heron, Ph.D.
Professor
Department of Human Services, Education
The Ohio State University
Columbus, Ohio

CONTENT CONSULTANTS

Robert T. Brown, M.D.
Assoc. Prof. Clinical
Pediatrics Dir., Section for
Adolescent Health The Ohio State Univ.
Children's Hosp. Columbus, Ohio

Henry D. Drew, Ph.D.
Chemist, U.S. FDA
Div. of Drug Analysis
St. Louis, Missouri

Judith L. Doyle, Ph.D.
Physics Teacher
Newark High School
Newark, Ohio

Todd F. Holzman, M.D.
Child Psychiatrist
Harvard Com. Health Plan
Wellesley, Massachusetts

Knut J. Norstog, Ph.D.
Research Associate
Fairchild Tropical Garden
Miami, Florida

James B. Phipps, Ph.D.
Prof., Geol./Oceanography
Grays Harbor College
Aberdeen, Washington

R. Robert Robbins, Ph.D.
Assoc. Professor
Astronomy Department
University of Texas
Austin, Texas

Sidney E. White, Ph.D.
Professor
Dept. of Geology/Mineralogy
The Ohio State Univ.
Columbus, Ohio

REVIEWERS: Teachers and Administrators

Joan Achen, General Herkimer Elementary School, Utica, NY; **Mary Alice Bernreuter,** Mae Walters Elementary School, Hialeah, FL; **Jack Finger,** Waukesha Public Schools, Waukesha, WI; **Sister Teresa Fitzgerald,** CSJ, Office of Catholic Education, Brooklyn, NY; **Janice Gritton,** Gravin H. Cochran Elementary School, Louisville, KY; **Ann Hanacik,** Blair Elementary School, Waukesha, WI; **Barbara Kmetz,** Trumbull High School, Trumbull, CT; **Waltina Mr'oczek,** Beachwood Elementary School, Beachwood, OH; **Edith Mueller,** Northview Elementary School, Waukesha, WI; **Peggy Smith,** Special Education Resource Teacher, Fort Worth, TX; **Frank Stone,** Floranada Elementary School, Fort Lauderdale, FL; **John Varine,** Kiski Area School District, Vandergrift, PA; **Sue Ann Whan,** Greece Central School District, Rochester, NY; **Dr. Rosa White,** Cutler Ridge Elementary School, Miami, FL

Table of Contents

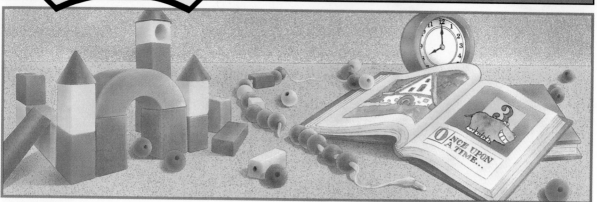

Activities

Activities

Process Skill Models

Problem Solving Activities

Science is...

Understanding

Understanding

"All my life through, the new sights of Nature made me rejoice like a child."

Marie Curie   French chemist (1867–1934)

What happens in a fire?
Where do things go when they dissolve?
How do skateboards work?
Science has some answers for you.

Science is... *Discovering*

"That's one small step for a man, one giant leap for mankind."
Neil A. Armstrong
American astronaut (July 21, 1969)

Neil Armstrong discovered what it was like to be the first person to step on the moon.

Discover science!

Science is...

Deciding

"Humans are unique because they have the capacity to choose what they do."
Richard E. Leakey
Kenyan palaeoanthropologist (1981)

You will make many choices today that affect your life and the lives of others. What choices will you make for tomorrow?

Science can help you decide.

Science is ... Applying

"I just invent, then wait until man comes around to needing what I've invented."

R. Buckminster Fuller
American engineer (1895–1983)

In about 1900, a Connecticut pie company found that people enjoyed playing catch with empty pie pans. Who ran the pie company? Joseph R. Frisbie! Have you thrown a Frisbee today?

Science is...

Measuring

Using
Numbers

Controlling Variables

Interpreting Data

Predicting

Hypothesizing

in your world...

Find out all about these
process skills on pages 333-343
of this science book.

Physical Science

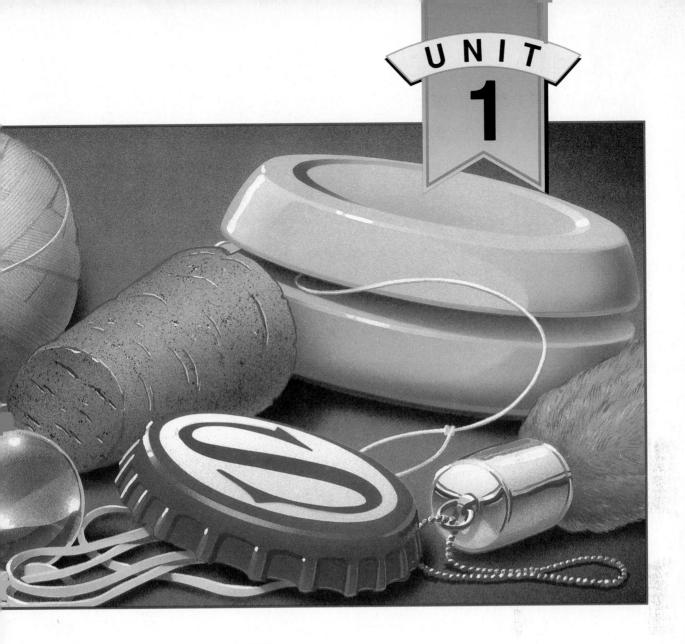

I keep bottle caps,
I keep string,
I keep keys and corks
And all such things.

from "Keepsakes"
Leland B. Jacobs

Think Like a Scientist

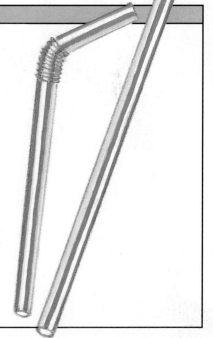

Have you ever had a drink of cold juice on a hot day? These children are both drinking juice, but the straws they are using are different. How are they different? Why does one child need a straw that bends?

ACTIVITY

Have You Ever...

Experimented With Straws?

Scientists are close observers. Look closely at a straight straw and a bendable straw. How are they different, and how are they the same? Scientists make changes to see what will happen. Make a change. Bend each straw. Try drinking out of each one and record what happens. Why do you think a bendable straw works? What part of your body bends like a bendable straw?

Using a Scientific Method

LESSON 1 GOALS
You will learn
● that people can use scientific methods to solve problems in everyday life.
● about the first steps in a scientific method.

Tony and his family were just finishing their supper. Tony was proud because he had helped cook. After dinner all of the family helped clear the dirty dishes. Tony and his sister Anne started washing the dishes. They were having trouble getting the greasy pots and pans clean. Anne said, "We should be using the new dish soap I saw advertised on TV. The TV ad said it's the best dish soap for greasy pots and pans!"

6

Tony's mother smiled and said, "Our dish soap is fine. Just get finished!"

Tony and Anne finished the pots and pans, while Tony thought, "They're probably pretty much the same. It probably doesn't matter which one we use." Still, Tony wondered if there was a way to find out which dish soap was really best.

Tony didn't realize it, but he was beginning to think like a scientist. **Scientific methods** are lists of steps that scientists use to solve problems. You, too, can use a scientific method to find the answers to everyday problems.

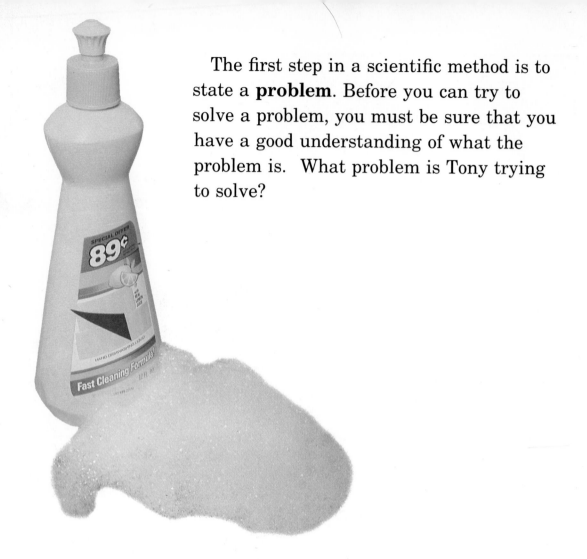

The first step in a scientific method is to state a **problem**. Before you can try to solve a problem, you must be sure that you have a good understanding of what the problem is. What problem is Tony trying to solve?

Lesson Summary

- Scientific methods are ways that scientists and other people use to solve problems.
- The first step in the scientific method is to state the problem.

Lesson Review

1. What do we call the lists of steps that scientists use to solve problems?
★2. Why would a scientist first state the problem?

How fast will sugar dissolve?

What you need

3 small, clear jars
(labeled A, B, and C)
measuring cup
water (ice, room temperature,
warm)
thermometer
3 sugar cubes
watch
pencil and paper

What to do

1. Pour 125 mL of ice water into cup A.
2. Pour 125 mL of room-temperature water into cup B and 125 mL of warm water into cup C.
3. Record the temperature of the water in each cup.
4. Guess which cup of water will dissolve the sugar cube first.
5. Drop a sugar cube into each cup.
6. Observe each cup for 10 minutes. Record your observations.

What did you learn?

1. In which cup did it take the longest time for the sugar to dissolve? the shortest?
2. How does water temperature affect the time needed to dissolve sugar?

Using what you learned

1. Would it be easier to make hot tea or iced tea sweet? Why?
2. What else might affect how long it takes to dissolve a sugar cube?

9

Setting Up an Experiment

LESSON 2 GOALS
You will learn
● that an experiment is used to test a hypothesis.
● that a variable is something in an experiment that can change.

On his way home from school the next day, Tony saw Mrs. Ortiz, who owns a flower shop. Today she was stirring something in a pail with a long spoon. "What are you doing?" asked Tony.

Mrs. Ortiz explained that she was mixing some plant food into water for the plants in her greenhouse. Tony asked why she was stirring the mixture. "It helps dissolve the plant food in the water," said Mrs. Ortiz. "Most things will dissolve faster if you stir them."

Tony thought about what Mrs. Ortiz said and asked, "Do you want to do an experiment?"

He explained that they were studying about scientific methods at school. First, they needed to state the problem they were trying to solve. Tony wrote the problem on a piece of paper.

Problem: How can we make plant food dissolve in water faster?

The second step in the scientific method is to guess a possible answer. It is important to set up an experiment to test if your guess is correct. A guess that can be tested with an experiment is called a **hypothesis** (hi PAHTH uh sus).

What is a hypothesis?

Mrs. Ortiz said, "We already have a hypothesis for our experiment." Tony wrote it down.

Hypothesis: Plant food will dissolve in water faster if we stir it.

Next, Tony and Mrs. Ortiz gathered their materials. They found two pails, a liter bottle, a thermometer, a tablespoon, the plant food, and the long spoon.

Tony poured exactly four liters of water into each pail. "It is important to have the same amount of water in each pail," said Mrs. Ortiz.

"Otherwise, it wouldn't be a fair test," said Tony.

"We should also make sure the water temperatures are the same," said Mrs. Ortiz. She used the thermometer to take the temperature of the water in each pail. She showed Tony how to read the thermometer. The temperature of the water in each pail was 18°C. Then they carefully added exactly one level tablespoon of plant food to each pail. Tony stirred one of the pails while Mrs. Ortiz timed him for five minutes. Tony looked in the pail he was stirring and saw that the plant food had dissolved. The plant food in the other pail could still be seen on the bottom. What did Tony and Mrs. Ortiz find out about their hypothesis?

After you state a problem and suggest a hypothesis, you decide on an experiment. The experiment must test whether or not your guess is correct. Things that change in an experiment are **variables**. The variable that Tony and Mrs. Ortiz changed was the stirring. The variable that they tested was how to make the plant food dissolve faster. The pail that they didn't stir was the control. A **control** shows what happens if nothing is changed in an experiment. Without a control, Tony wouldn't know if stirring did any good. The plant food dissolved in the pail that Tony stirred. What about the plant food in the control—the plant food that he didn't stir?

What is a control?

PLANT FOOD

There are other possible variables that Tony could test. It is important to test only one variable at a time. For example, the temperature of the water could be a variable. What would have happened if Tony did not have water of the same temperature in each pail?

How many variables should you test at a time?

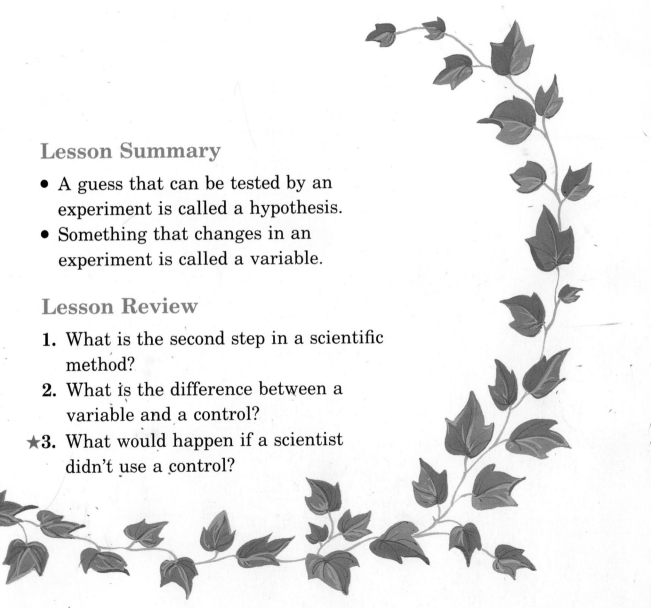

Lesson Summary

- A guess that can be tested by an experiment is called a hypothesis.
- Something that changes in an experiment is called a variable.

Lesson Review

1. What is the second step in a scientific method?
2. What is the difference between a variable and a control?
★3. What would happen if a scientist didn't use a control?

Recording and Discussing Data

LESSON 3 GOALS
You will learn
● that the results of an experiment can be compared to a control.
● that a chart can help you show the results of an experiment.

Tony and Mrs. Ortiz talked about their experiment. Tony said, "In school I learned how to make a record of the results of an experiment. I'll write down the results tonight and show them to you tomorrow."

When Tony got home, he told his mother about the experiment. They worked together and made a chart that looked like this:

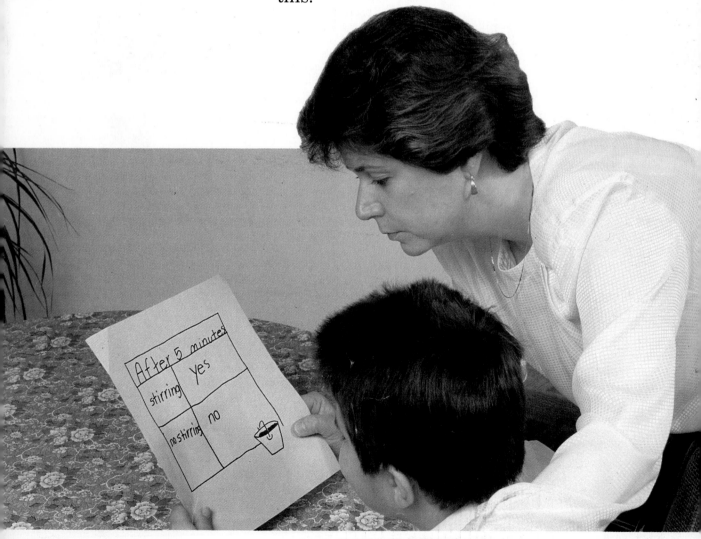

You Can...

Make a Chart

Scientists must know how to organize their data. One way to organize data is to use a chart. This chart shows how the height of two plants changed. You can make your own chart. Talk to ten friends. Find out how many brothers and sisters each friend has. Put your data into a chart. Who has the most brothers? sisters?

Height of Plants

Day	Plant A	Plant B
1	5 cm	5 cm
2	$5\frac{1}{2}$ cm	6 cm
3	6 cm	7 cm
4	$6\frac{1}{2}$ cm	7 cm
5	7 cm	9 cm

Looking at his results, Tony could tell that his hypothesis seemed to be correct. He thought about other variables. He wondered how long it would take the plant food to dissolve in warm water. He decided to try another experiment with Mrs. Ortiz.

For one of the last steps of the scientific method, you must make a record of your results. It may also help if you discuss the results of your experiment with others. A chart can help you think about the results of an experiment. Finally, you need to decide whether or not the results support your hypothesis. If the results do not support your hypothesis, you may want to make another guess and design a new experiment to test your new guess.

SCIENCE AND . . .

Reading

What do you think will happen when Tony and Mrs. Ortiz add plant food to warm water? The plant food will
A. dissolve slower.
B. dissolve faster.
C. not dissolve.

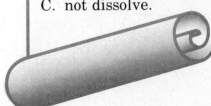

Many times when you think about the results of an experiment, you will think of other experiments to try. That is what happened to Tony when he looked at his results.

At dinner that night, Tony suggested that they try the scientific method to solve the problem of finding the best dish soap for greasy pots and pans. Tony's father said he would buy different kinds of dish soap at the grocery store. They talked about the variables, controls, and possible hypotheses.

The next night after dinner, it was time to experiment. Tony's father had bought two bottles of dish soap, the one Anne had seen on TV and a store-brand bottle. They also decided to test the one they already had at home.

It was hard to decide how to test the soap. They finally decided to rub a teaspoonful of grease on three spoons and stir the spoons in bowls filled with each type of soap and water. Anne's hypothesis was that the soap she saw on TV would clean the spoon fastest. Tony didn't think the kind of soap would make any difference. He thought all the soaps would clean the spoons with the same number of stirs.

Would You Believe?

People's tongue prints are as unique as their fingerprints.

They measured the same amount of soap into each bowl. Then they mixed in the same amount of water. They checked the temperature of the water in each bowl to make sure it was the same. They noticed that the store-brand soap did not seem to make as many suds as the other two. Then they began to stir the greasy spoons. They checked the spoons after each stir. When all the grease was gone from each spoon, they wrote down the number of stirs that it had taken.

After they collected their results, Tony and Anne made a chart like the one below. They found out that both of their hypotheses were wrong. Mother had been correct! Maybe they had been using the best dish soap all along!

	Number of stirs
Soap 1 – TV	11 stirs
Soap 2 – Store brand	10 stirs
Soap 3 – Mother's	7 stirs

Lesson Summary

- The results of an experiment must be compared with the hypothesis.
- A chart can help you compare the results of an experiment.

Lesson Review

1. What is the last step of a scientific method?
★2. Why would you want to discuss the results of the experiment with someone?

How can you find the best soap?

What you need

3 margarine tubs with lids
(labeled A, B, and C)
3 brands liquid dish soap
(labeled A, B, and C)
3 droppers
warm water
measuring cup
vegetable oil
small spoon
pencil and paper

What to do

1. Put 1 drop of soap A into tub A. Do the same with the other soaps and tubs.
2. Guess which soap would best clean greasy dishes.
3. Slowly add 125 mL of water to each tub.
4. Put the lids on the tubs and swirl them around.
5. Describe the suds in each tub.
6. Add 1 spoonful of oil to each tub. Repeat steps 4–5.

7. Repeat steps 4–6 until you have added 5 spoonfuls of oil to each tub. Record your observations after each spoonful.

What did you learn?

1. Which soap had the most suds after step 4?
2. What happened to the suds as you added more oil?

Using what you learned

1. Which soap would be best for washing greasy dishes?
2. If all soaps cost the same, which will probably be cheapest to use?

I WANT TO KNOW ABOUT...

Taking Notes

A detective is a person who searches for information that is not easy to find. A detective must investigate or find out information. He or she must closely study facts already known and ask questions to get all the information that is needed. A detective, while observing or asking questions, writes notes. These notes are important. They are the written record of what the detective has seen or heard.

A detective is like a doctor. A doctor observes or listens to a patient and records information. All information is then on hand when the doctor decides what is wrong with the patient.

As a student, you should work in the same way as a detective or doctor. You should observe, study, ask questions, and take notes. When you get ready to review, the notes can help you remember what you have already read or observed.

Language Arts

Summary

Lesson 1
- Scientific methods are used every day to solve problems.
- The first step in the scientific method is to state a problem.

Lesson 2
- An experiment is used to test a hypothesis.

- A variable is something in an experiment that changes.

Lesson 3
- The results of an experiment are compared to the hypothesis.
- A chart helps to compare the results of an experiment.

Science Words

Fill in the blank with the correct word or words from the list.

scientific methods
problem　　　　　**variables**
hypothesis　　　　**control**

1. A guess that can be tested by an experiment is a(n) ___ .
2. The first step in a scientific method is to state a(n) ___ .
3. Things in an experiment that change are called ___ .
4. The pail that Tony didn't stir was the ___ .

5. Lists of steps scientists use to solve problems are ___ .

Questions

Recalling Ideas

Correctly complete each of the following sentences.

1. The second step in a scientific method is to state a(n)
   - (a) problem.
   - (b) hypothe- sis.
   - (c) control.
   - (d) experiment.
2. After you state a problem and suggest a hypothesis, you then decide on a(n)
   - (a) observa- tion.
   - (b) control.
   - (c) experiment.
   - (d) variable.
3. How many variables should be tested at one time?
   - (a) one
   - (b) four
   - (c) three
   - (d) two
4. In the experiment with the two pails of water, the pail that was stirred was the
   - (a) control.
   - (b) variable.
   - (c) experiment.
   - (d) hypothesis.

Understanding Ideas

Answer the following questions using complete sentences.

1. Why should you state the problem before doing an experiment?

2. Why is it important to test only one variable at a time?
3. What might you do if your result doesn't support your hypothesis?
4. Why should you make a record of your results?

Thinking Critically

Think about what you have learned in this chapter. Answer the following questions using complete sentences.

1. Imagine that you are testing the effect of water on growing radish seeds. You plant 5 seeds in each of 10 different plots. The first plot gets only rain. Each remaining plot gets a little more water than the one before. After 5 days, count how many seeds have sprouted in each plot. What were the variables? What was the control?
2. Name an everyday problem you could study using scientific methods. Think of a hypothesis and a way to test it.

SCIENCE
In Your World

Matter

Everything around us takes up space. These children are trying to fit something into a space that is already filled. Papers and leaves use the space in the garbage can, so the bag will not fit.

ACTIVITY

Have You Ever...

Experimented With the Space in a Cup?

Fill the cup with water. Put it on a paper towel. What do you think will happen when you try to put something else into the space that is filled with water? Try it and see. Put a marble in the cup. What happens? What do you think will happen if you put another marble in the cup? Why do you think it will happen?

Properties of Objects

LESSON 1 GOALS

You will learn
● that properties describe objects.
● the two properties that are common to all objects.
● two of the units used to measure mass.

Have you ever played soccer? A soccer ball is different from a basketball or a volleyball. Suppose you are sent to get a soccer ball. In the gym storage room, you will find many kinds of balls. Some are big and some are little. Some are made of plastic, some of leather, and some seem to be covered with soft fuzz. Some are white, some are brown, and some have more than one color. Some are soft and some are hard. Some are not even round! How will you choose the right ball?

Objects have properties.

28

We describe objects in many ways. Size and shape are used to describe objects. Color and smoothness or roughness can also be used to describe objects. Size, shape, color, smoothness, and roughness are some properties of objects. A **property** (PRAHP urt ee) is a characteristic of an object. What are some properties of the soccer ball you have been sent to get? How can you use properties to find the right kind of ball?

ACTIVITY

You Can...

Sort the Shoes

Work with a team of five other students. Each team member puts one shoe in a pile. Have a team member use one property to put the shoes into two groups. Take turns guessing that property. The first person to guess correctly then groups the shoes based on another property. Keep going until each team member has had a turn. What properties did members of your team use to group the shoes?

You have to find a leather ball with black and white patches on it. Be sure to choose one that's hard so you know it's full of air. You use the properties of all the balls in the storage room to choose exactly the right one.

Now look at the pictures of balls. The balls are all different. All of them, however, are alike in two ways. First, all of them take up space. No two balls can be in the same place at the same time.

Second, all of the balls have mass. **Mass** is how much there is of an object. A bowling ball, for example, has more mass than a softball. The softball has more mass than a table tennis ball.

What is mass?

Objects have mass and take up space.

Small masses are measured in grams.

You can measure the mass of objects. One unit we use to measure mass is the gram. One **gram** is a very small amount of mass. Two paper clips have a mass of about one gram. A nickel has a mass of about five grams.

Sometimes you may want to measure a large mass. Large amounts of mass can be measured in kilograms (KEE luh grams). A **kilogram** is 1,000 grams. The mass of a large dump truck is about 10,000 kilograms. The mass of a baby is 4 kilograms. What do you think your mass is?

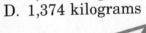

SCIENCE AND . . .

Math

The mass of which of the following mid-size cars has a 4 in the hundreds place and a 7 in the ones place?
A. 1,534 kilograms
B. 1,724 kilograms
C. 1,437 kilograms
D. 1,374 kilograms

When choosing between two items, you can use the properties of objects to help you make decisions.

Lesson Summary

- A property is a characteristic of an object.
- All objects take up space and have mass.
- Two units used to measure mass are the gram and the kilogram.

Lesson Review

1. What are two properties of all objects?
2. What is the mass of one nickel?
★3. Would you use paper clips to measure the mass of a person? Why or why not?

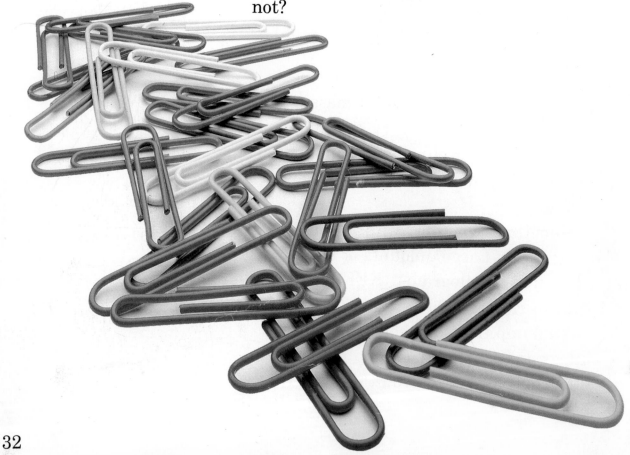

How do you measure mass?

What you need

10 nickels
20 paper clips
balance
4 small objects
pencil and paper

What to do

1. Predict the mass of each object in nickels and in paper clips.
2. Write your predictions on a chart. Start with the object you predict has the most mass.
3. Put 1 object on the left side of the balance. Place nickels and paper clips on the right side until both pans are balanced.
4. Record the number of nickels and paper clips used.
5. Repeat steps 3 and 4 for the other objects.

What did you learn?

1. How many of your predictions were correct?
2. Which object has the most mass?

Using what you learned

1. How can you find the mass for each object in grams? Try it.
2. When would it be hard to find the mass of objects using nickels and paper clips?

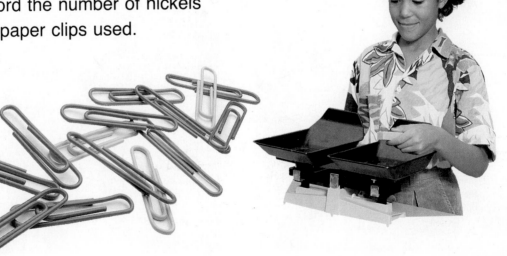

What Is Matter?

Take just one minute to list as many things around you as possible. How many things did you list?

All of the things you listed are the same in one way. They all are matter.

Everything that takes up space and has mass is called **matter.** Rocks, clocks, bees, and trees are matter. Everything around you is made of matter. You are made of matter, too.

Matter can be a solid, a liquid, or a gas. The pictures on this page show matter that is solid, liquid, and gas.

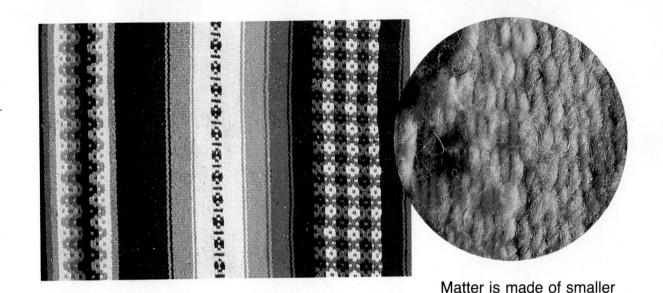

Matter is made of smaller parts.

From far away, the blanket in the picture looks as if it is all one piece. As you get closer, however, you see that the blanket is made of many small threads woven together. How might you get a good view of each separate thread?

Each thread in the blanket is made of even smaller parts. The small parts are called atoms. An **atom** is the smallest part of any kind of matter. Remember that all matter is the same in some ways. All matter has mass and takes up space. This is also true of atoms. Atoms have mass and take up space.

What is an atom?

You Can...

Find the Smallest Part

When is a carrot no longer a carrot? See if you can keep cutting a cooked carrot into smaller and smaller pieces. When you think the carrot can't be cut anymore, use a fork to mash what is left. Stop when you think the carrot is no longer a carrot. What is your reason for thinking the carrot has changed?

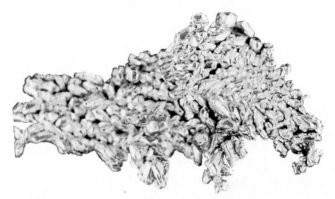

Matter made of only one kind of atom is called an **element.** You probably already know of some elements. For example, gold is an element. Gold is made of gold atoms. No other element contains gold atoms. The properties of elements are different because they are made of different kinds of atoms.

Gold is an element.

36

Lesson Summary

- Everything that takes up space and has mass is called matter.
- An atom is the smallest part of any kind of matter.
- An element is made of only one kind of atom.

Lesson Review

1. What is an element?
★2. Is a shadow matter? Why or why not?

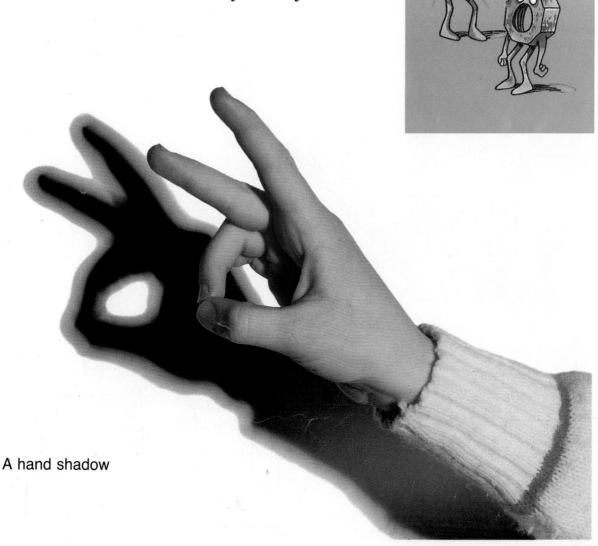

A hand shadow

States of Matter

LESSON 3 GOALS
You will learn
● the properties of solids.
● the properties of liquids.
● that some matter has properties of both solids and liquids.
● the properties of gases.

You remember from Lesson 1 that some properties of objects are size, shape, color, smoothness, and roughness. Now you'll see how the properties of an object can show the object's state of matter.

Wood, milk, and air have different properties. They are put in different groups because of their different properties. Wood is a solid, milk is a liquid, and air is a gas. Matter can be grouped by whether it is a solid, a liquid, or a gas. Solids, liquids, and gases are states of matter.

What are the groupings of matter as solids, liquids, and gases called?

Wood is a solid. A **solid** is matter that has a certain size and shape. Most of the objects you see are in the solid state. Your desk is a solid. It does not change its shape or size.

Atoms are particles of matter. Solids, liquids, and gases are all made up of particles of matter. Particles of matter are always moving. How much the particles are moving tells the state of the matter—solid, liquid, or gas.

In a solid, the particles are packed closely together in a definite pattern. The particles can only shake. They can't move out of their pattern. Solids don't change shape because of the pattern of the particles in them.

Solids don't change size or shape.

Milk is a liquid (LIHK wud). A **liquid** is matter that has a certain size or volume but does not have a shape of its own. A liquid takes the shape of its container. Look at the picture of the milk. What shape is the milk in the pitcher? What shape is the same milk in the glass?

Liquids flow. They can be poured. You can pour milk from a pitcher into a glass. Liquids also have a certain volume. When you pour milk from a small carton into a tall glass, the shape of the milk changes, but the amount of milk is still the same.

Liquids are also made of particles. The particles in liquids move more freely than those in solids. Particles in liquids fall over each other and don't form a definite pattern. Liquids pour and change shape because of the way their particles move.

What can change in a liquid? What can't change?

Liquids change shape.

40

Some matter has properties of both liquids and solids. This kind of matter seems to have a definite shape as solids do. However, its particles don't form a definite pattern. This kind of matter may even change shape slowly over time.

Look at the picture of butter. Cold butter has a definite shape and volume. Now think about spreading butter on warm toast. As the butter warms, it gets softer and softer. Soon it flows like a liquid, doesn't it? So butter has some properties of both solids and liquids.

A gelatin dessert is also like a solid and a liquid. It has a definite mass. It keeps its shape, but its particles are not in a pattern. That explains why its shape can easily be changed. What other matter can you think of that has some properties of both solids and liquids?

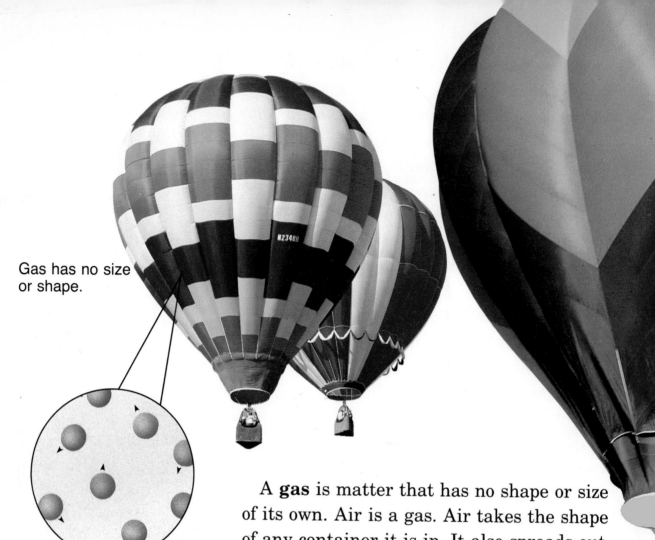

Gas has no size or shape.

What state of matter is air?

A **gas** is matter that has no shape or size of its own. Air is a gas. Air takes the shape of any container it is in. It also spreads out to fill any size container. Air particles can spread out to fill a large container such as a barrel. The same amount of air can also be put into a smaller container such as a jar. What would happen to the space between particles when air is moved from a large to a small container?

Gas particles move very freely. They are also farther apart from each other than the particles of a liquid or a solid. The particles of a gas spread out to fill any container. The same amount of gas can fill a small jar or a large room.

States of matter

Lesson Summary

- Solid matter has a certain size and shape.
- Liquid matter has a certain size but doesn't have a shape of its own.
- Some matter has properties of both solids and liquids.
- Matter that is a gas doesn't have a size or shape of its own.

Lesson Review

1. What are three states of matter?
2. Matter in which state does not easily change its shape?
3. Which state of matter can spread to fill any size container?
★4. How are the properties of solids and liquids alike? How are they different?

Is it a solid or a liquid?

What you need

newspaper
paper cup
"mystery matter"
paper towels
pencil and paper

What to do

1. Cover your desk with newspaper.
2. Get a cup of "mystery matter" from your teacher.
3. Carefully test the "mystery matter." Try the following things:
   (a) Try to pour it.
   (b) Poke it with your fingers.

Test	Observations
Pouring "mystery matter"	
Poking "mystery matter"	
Rolling "mystery matter"	
Other	

(c) Roll it into a ball and try to bounce it on the desk.
4. Make a chart like the one above and record your observations.

What did you learn?

1. How was the "mystery matter" like a solid?
2. How was it like a liquid?

Using what you learned

1. What properties of butter make it like the "mystery matter"?
2. Gelatin, glass, and peanut butter are also like the "mystery matter." How does temperature make them more like a liquid or a solid?

44

I WANT TO KNOW ABOUT...

A Hot-Air Balloonist

George McCall is a hot-air balloonist. He and a friend are preparing a hot-air balloon for takeoff. Before this can happen, George must inflate the balloon. He turns on a burner to heat the air in the balloon. Heated air is lighter than the same amount of cooler air.

The inflated balloon is about seven stories high. The balloon is made of light, strong nylon covered with a thin plastic coating. The nylon holds the heated air in the balloon. A basket called a gondola hangs under the balloon. This is where George and his friend will ride. Heavy bags of sand, tied to the gondola, help keep the balloon on the ground.

Everything is now ready. George and his friend climb into the gondola. They untie the sand bags and leave them on the ground. The inflated balloon and gondola rise into the air.

George and his friend don't feel as if they are moving. But they see that the trees and houses are getting farther and farther away. The balloon drifts with the wind. After a while the air in the balloon cools. George turns on the burner to heat the air and keep the balloon up. When George wants to land, he releases some of the heated air. Slowly they drift to Earth, and the ride is over for the day.

Career

Summary

Lesson 1
- A property is a characteristic of an object.
- All objects take up space and have mass.
- The gram and kilogram are used to measure mass.

Lesson 2
- Matter is anything around you that takes up space and has mass.
- All matter is made of atoms.

- An element is made of only one kind of atom.

Lesson 3
- Solid matter has a certain size and shape.
- Liquid matter has a certain size but not a certain shape.
- Some matter has properties of both solids and liquids.
- Matter that is a gas has no size or shape of its own.

Science Words

Fill in the blank with the correct word or words from the list.

mass	atom	kilograms	liquid	property
matter	element	solid	gas	gram

1. Matter that has no shape or size of its own is called a(n) ___.

2. All objects that have mass and take up space are ___.

3. A(n) ___ is made of only one kind of atom.

4. A(n) ___ has a certain size but no shape of its own.

5. Matter that has a certain size and shape is called a(n) ___.

6. The smallest part of matter is called a(n) ___.

7. How much there is of an object is called ___.

Questions

Recalling Ideas

Correctly complete each of the following sentences.

1. Particles move least freely in
   (a) grams.
   (c) liquids.
   (b) solids.
   (d) gases.
2. A person's mass is best measured in
   (a) atoms.
   (c) kilograms.
   (b) Celsius.
   (d) properties.
3. A characteristic of an object is a(n)
   (a) atom.
   (c) property.
   (b) element.
   (d) matter.
4. Matter is made of
   (a) grams.
   (c) patterns.
   (b) liquids.
   (d) atoms.

5. A softball has less mass than a
   (a) bowling ball.
   (c) feather.
   (b) tennis ball.
   (d) pin.
6. The unit used to measure the masses of very small objects is the
   (a) element.
   (c) atom.
   (b) gram.
   (d) kilogram.

Understanding Ideas

Answer the following questions using complete sentences.

1. What are two properties that all matter has?
2. Why are there so many kinds of matter?

Thinking Critically

Think about what you have learned in this chapter. Answer the following questions using complete sentences.

1. Most gases cannot be seen. How do we know they are there?
2. How is a crayon like both a solid and a liquid?

3

Changes in Matter

When you walk in the rain, raindrops on your raincoat look clearer than water in puddles. How does water change when it falls on the ground? How does the ground change when it gets wet?

ACTIVITY

Have You Ever...

Seen Matter Changing?

You will need two jars about half filled with water. You should also have about 50 g of dirt and 50 g of salt. Observe the water, the dirt, and the salt. Record your observations. Then pour the dirt into one jar and the salt into another. Stir the mixtures. How has each kind of matter changed? Record your observations. Do you think you could separate the dirt or the salt from the water? How?

Changing Matter

LESSON 1 GOALS
You will learn
● that the properties of matter can change.
● that matter can expand and contract.
● why heat causes matter to expand.

Have you ever helped build a doghouse? Maybe you helped with sanding the wood smooth, or perhaps you helped with the painting. If you worked carefully, the changes you made helped the doghouse to look its best.

In working with wood, you caused some of the properties of the wood to change. Color, size, shape, smoothness, and roughness are some physical properties of matter. Physical properties of matter can be used to tell how matter looks or feels. A change in a physical property is called a **physical change.** What physical change are the people in the picture with the doghouse causing?

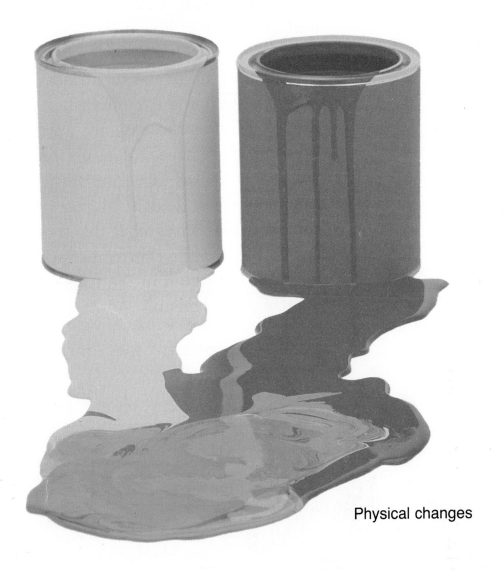

Physical changes

You can break, bend, tear, or stretch some solids. When a solid is broken, bent, torn, or stretched, its shape is changed.

The physical properties of a liquid or a gas can also be changed. Look at the picture of the paint on this page. How have the properties of the matter—that is, the paint—changed?

How can you change the shape of a solid?

Heat can cause a physical change of matter. Think of how a thermometer works. When a thermometer is in a warm area, the liquid in the tube rises. It rises because the liquid expands when it is heated. Matter that expands gets bigger. It takes up more space. Most matter expands when it is heated. Most matter also contracts when it cools. Matter that contracts gets smaller. It takes up less space. Look at the thermometer on this page. If the liquid in the tube contracts, what would it mean?

Liquid expands

Air expands

SCIENCE AND . . .

Reading

What is the main idea of this lesson?
A. Students like to run on playgrounds.
B. People do not like cracks in the roads.
C. Heat causes matter to expand.
D. Thermometers cause matter to change.

Matter expands because heat makes the particles of matter move faster. As they move faster, the particles move farther apart. This movement makes the matter expand. When a car is driven for a long time, the tires get hot. What do you think happens to the air in those tires?

Sometimes problems take place when matter expands. Concrete in roads may expand and crack in hot weather. Naturally, people want to stop the roads from cracking. To solve the problem of concrete cracking, some roads are built with tar strips between the sections of concrete. The soft tar moves out of the way to allow the concrete to expand. That means there is less chance that the concrete will crack.

Why is tar placed between sections of concrete?

There are many ways to cause physical changes of matter. How are the boys in the picture making physical changes to matter?

Changing physical properties

Lesson Summary

- Size, shape, color, and smoothness of matter can be changed.
- Heat causes matter to expand.
- Matter contracts when it cools.

Lesson Review

1. What are some physical properties that can be changed?
2. What happens to most matter when it is cooled?
★3. How does heat cause matter to expand?

54

How can you make a dime dance?

What you need

soft-drink bottle
freezer
safety goggles
dropper
dime
pencil and paper

What to do

1. Place the empty bottle in the freezer for 30 minutes.
2. Put on the safety goggles.
3. Put the cold bottle on a table. Using the dropper, place a few drops of water on the rim of the bottle.
4. Cover the mouth of the bottle with a dime.
5. Watch the dime and the bottle for a few minutes and record your observations.

Test	Observations
1 minute	
3 minutes	
5 minutes	
7 minutes	

What did you learn?

1. What happened to the dime?
2. What happened to the air in the bottle?

Using what you learned

1. From the results of this activity, how do you know that air is matter?
2. How is what happened to the air in the bottle similar to how a thermometer works?

Changing States of Matter

LESSON 2 GOALS
You will learn
● that heat may cause matter to change state.
● the difference between melting and freezing.
● the difference between evaporation and condensation.

What if you want juice for breakfast? You open a can of frozen juice, but the juice does not pour. Disappointed, you leave the can on the counter for a while. Later you try to pour the juice again. This time the juice pours easily. Why could you pour the juice the second time you tried?

You already learned that adding or losing heat causes matter to expand or contract. Now you will see that heat may also cause matter to change its state. Where did the heat come from that melted the frozen juice? When things get hotter or colder, they can melt or freeze. Things melt when they change from solids to liquids. Things freeze when they change from liquids to solids.

Heat changes matter

You Can...

Win the Ice Cube Race

Think of different ways to melt an ice cube. Choose the way that you predict will be the fastest. Gather any materials you need and try the method you chose. Remember to record how long it takes for your ice cube to melt. Compare your results with those of your classmates. Which method worked best? What was the shortest time?

When matter gains or loses heat, the matter can change state. When solids melt, they change to the liquid state. The solid frozen orange juice gained heat when it melted. On the other hand, liquids freeze when they change to the solid state. Liquids lose heat when they freeze.

Remember from Lesson 3 in Chapter 2 what the particles in solids look like. They are arranged into a definite pattern. Even though all particles move, the particles in solids move the least. They can only shake back and forth or up and down in their places. They stay in their patterns, and they don't change shape.

What word describes the change of matter from the solid state to the liquid state?

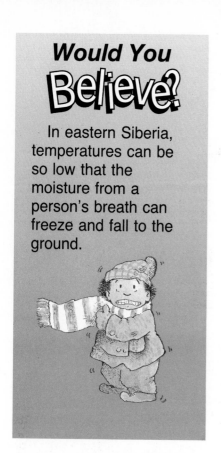
Now ask yourself, "When a solid melts into a liquid, what are the particles doing?" Remember that solids gain heat to melt. The added heat makes the particles in the solids move faster. Heat also makes the particles move apart. The pattern that the particles had been in breaks down. The particles begin moving past each other. As the pattern breaks down, the solids change to liquids. You may have seen ice change to liquid water. Most solids melt if enough heat is added.

When liquids freeze, they change to the solid state. Liquids freeze when enough heat is removed from them. As heat is lost, the particles of liquid matter move more slowly. They move closer together. When the particles form a definite pattern, the liquid has become a solid.

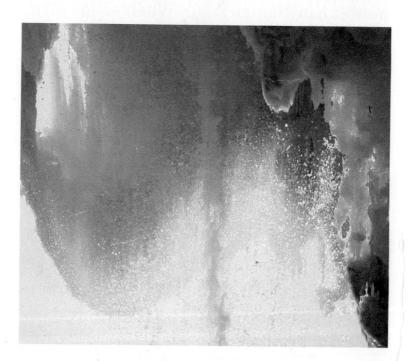

Solids melt

Liquids can also change to gases. Remember that particles of liquids move from place to place. They bump into each other. The particles on the top layer of a liquid may be bumped away from the rest of the liquid. These particles become a gas. This change from a liquid to a gas is called **evaporation** (ih vap uh RAY shun).

What is the change from a liquid to a gas called?

Water evaporates

After people wash their clothes, they use dryers or hang the clothes outside to dry. In the dryer or outdoors, warm temperatures speed evaporation. Although liquids can evaporate at any temperature, adding heat makes them evaporate faster. Why do you think this is true?

Sometimes a gas may lose heat. As the gas cools, its particles slow down and move closer together. The gas can change to a liquid. The change from a gas to a liquid is called **condensation** (kahn den SAY shun). Water will form on a glass of iced tea on a warm day. The cold glass causes some of the water that is a gas in the air to condense on the glass. Where have you seen other examples of a gas condensing?

Gases condense

Lesson Summary

- Adding heat may change matter from the solid state to the liquid state. Removing heat may change matter from the liquid state to the solid state.
- Evaporation is the change of matter from a liquid to a gas. Condensation is the change of matter from a gas to a liquid.

Lesson Review

1. What happens to the speed and pattern of particles of matter when heat is added to a solid? to a liquid?
2. What may happen when heat is removed from a liquid? from a gas?
★3. What happens to particles of gas during condensation?

How does water change?

What you need

baking dish
water
tape
plastic wrap
paper cup
pencil and paper

What to do

1. Place the dish by a window.
2. Fill the dish half full of water.
3. Cover the dish tightly with plastic wrap.
4. Tape the plastic wrap to the dish. Predict what will happen.
5. Observe the dish each day for 2 days.
6. Record your observations.

What did you learn?

1. What happened to the total amount of water in the covered dish?
2. What happened to the plastic wrap?
3. What changes did you observe between the first and second day?

Using what you learned

1. What caused the changes?
2. What do you think would happen if you took the plastic wrap off the dish? Try it and find out.
3. How does this activity show why bathroom mirrors sometimes become foggy?

Combining Matter

LESSON 3 GOALS
You will learn
● the properties of a mixture.
● the properties of a compound.
● that a chemical change takes place when a compound is formed.

In the picture on this page, the boy is counting money. There are different kinds of coins mixed in the pile. As he counts the coins, the boy separates them. The pile of coins is a mixture of different types of matter. The coins are not changed by mixing them together. They can be separated after they are mixed. Matter that is mixed together without changing the properties of each type of matter is called a **mixture.**

There are many mixtures. A fruit salad is a mixture. Different amounts of each fruit can be added to a salad. The properties of each fruit, however, do not change. The pieces of fruit can be separated after they are mixed.

Separating mixtures

However, not all mixtures can be taken apart as easily as a pile of coins or a fruit salad. For example, you can make a mixture called salt water if you mix table salt with water. Salt water doesn't look like a mixture. But it is a mixture, and it can be separated. You simply evaporate the water, and the salt is left behind.

Iron rusts

Different elements can be combined in such a way that they can't be easily separated later. Instead of mixtures we call them compounds. A **compound** is a kind of matter formed from two or more elements. The properties of a compound are different from the properties of the elements that make it up. A **chemical change** takes place when a compound forms.

Rust is a compound. A chemical change takes place when the elements iron and oxygen combine to form rust. The properties of rust are not the same as the properties of either iron or oxygen.

What kind of change takes place when a compound is formed?

Use Application Activity on pages 345, 346.

63

New compounds form when something burns. When wood burns, most of the elements in the wood combine with oxygen in the air. What new compounds are formed when wood burns?

Lesson Summary

- A mixture is different kinds of matter mixed together. In a mixture, each type of matter keeps its own properties.
- A compound is a combination of elements that is not a mixture. A compound has different properties than those of the elements from which it is made.
- A chemical change takes place when a compound is formed.

Lesson Review

1. Why is a salad a mixture?
2. Give an example of a compound.
★3. What kind of change takes place when a piece of wood is burned?

New compounds form

I WANT TO KNOW ABOUT...

Making Diamonds

Carol Lee makes diamonds. The diamonds are not used for jewelry, but they are used in industries. Diamonds are made from carbon. It normally takes Mother Nature millions of years to form a diamond. Carol, however, makes diamonds every day in her lab.

In the first step, Carol mixes carbon with some metals. She heats the mixture to a temperature of about 1,300°C. The mixture is put under great pressure. The mixture melts, and the carbon becomes diamond. When it cools, each diamond is cleaned.

Artificial diamonds are used in many ways. Large, high-quality diamonds are used on saws for cutting rocks and on drill bits for oil wells.

Small, imperfect artificial diamonds are combined with other materials to polish the edges of people's glasses and car windows. Carol says that in many cases her diamonds are better than natural diamonds.

Science and Technology

Summary

Lesson 1
- Properties of matter can be changed.
- Adding or removing heat can cause matter to expand or contract.

Lesson 2
- Matter may change state when heat is added or taken away.
- Solids melt when they change to liquids, and liquids freeze when they change to solids.

- The change from a liquid to a gas is evaporation, and the change from a gas to a liquid is condensation.

Lesson 3
- Matter that is mixed together but keeps its own properties is called a mixture.
- A compound has properties different from the elements that make it up.
- A chemical change takes place when a compound is formed.

Science Words

Fill in the blank with the correct word or words from the list.

evaporation   compound   mixture
condensation   physical change chemical change

1. To form a compound, a ____ takes place.
2. The change from a liquid to a gas is called ____ .

3. The change from a gas to a liquid is called ____ .
4. Matter that is formed from two or more elements is a(n) ____ .

Questions

Recalling Ideas

Correctly complete each of the following sentences.

1. When rust forms, the kind of change that takes place is
   (a) state.   (c) chemical.
   (b) physical. (d) evaporation.

2. An example of a common mixture is
   (a) oxygen.   (c) rust.
   (b) fruit salad. (d) salt.

3. Evaporation speeds up when liquids are exposed to
   (a) heat.   (c) condensation.
   (b) expansion. (d) cold.

Understanding Ideas

Answer the following questions using complete sentences.

1. Name two ways that heat changes matter.

2. Name a solid, liquid, and gas and tell how the physical properties of each can be changed.

3. What may happen to pavement in hot weather?

4. What happens to liquid when it freezes?

5. Describe the process of evaporation.

6. What happens to gas when it condenses?

Thinking Critically

Think about what you have learned in this chapter. Answer the following questions using complete sentences.

1. Why would people pour hot water on tight jar lids?

2. You are cooking stew. There is too much liquid in the pan. Why do you take the cover off the pan?

Forces and Work

On a windy day, you may notice that walking is more difficult when the wind blows against you. Can you think of other times when the wind makes you work harder? Are there times when the wind makes your work easier?

ACTIVITY

Have You Ever...

Compared How Objects Move?

Some things move more easily than others. If you think like a scientist, you can discover more about the wind and moving objects. Collect a wooden block, a marble, a crumpled ball of paper, and a pencil. Try to blow each one across the floor. Which are easier to move? Try testing other objects. What properties do you think make an object easy or difficult to move by wind?

Force

LESSON 1 GOALS
You will learn
● what is needed to move objects.
● that the amount of force needed to move an object depends on the object's mass.

We can move objects in different ways. Many objects will move if you push them. Other objects move when you pull them. A push or a pull is a **force.** The children at the playground swings are using forces. They are using pushes and pulls.

An object moves when you lift it. Lifting is a force. Do you use a push or a pull to lift a chair off the floor? Some objects can be lifted by using a small force. Other objects need greater force to be lifted. The amount of force needed to lift or move an object depends on how much matter the object has. Another way to say it is that the force needed depends on the object's mass.

Using pushes and pulls

70

Imagine you and a friend are helping to clear away the trash from an empty lot. It will make a good playground when the bricks and branches are cleared away. You fill two wheelbarrows with trash. One wheelbarrow has mostly bricks. The other has mostly branches. Both wheelbarrows are the same size. But the wheelbarrow full of bricks takes more force to push. That is because the wheelbarrow of bricks has more mass than the wheelbarrow of branches.

More force is needed to lift an object with a large mass. Look at the picture below. It would take more force to lift the bowling ball than the soccer ball. Which ball has more mass?

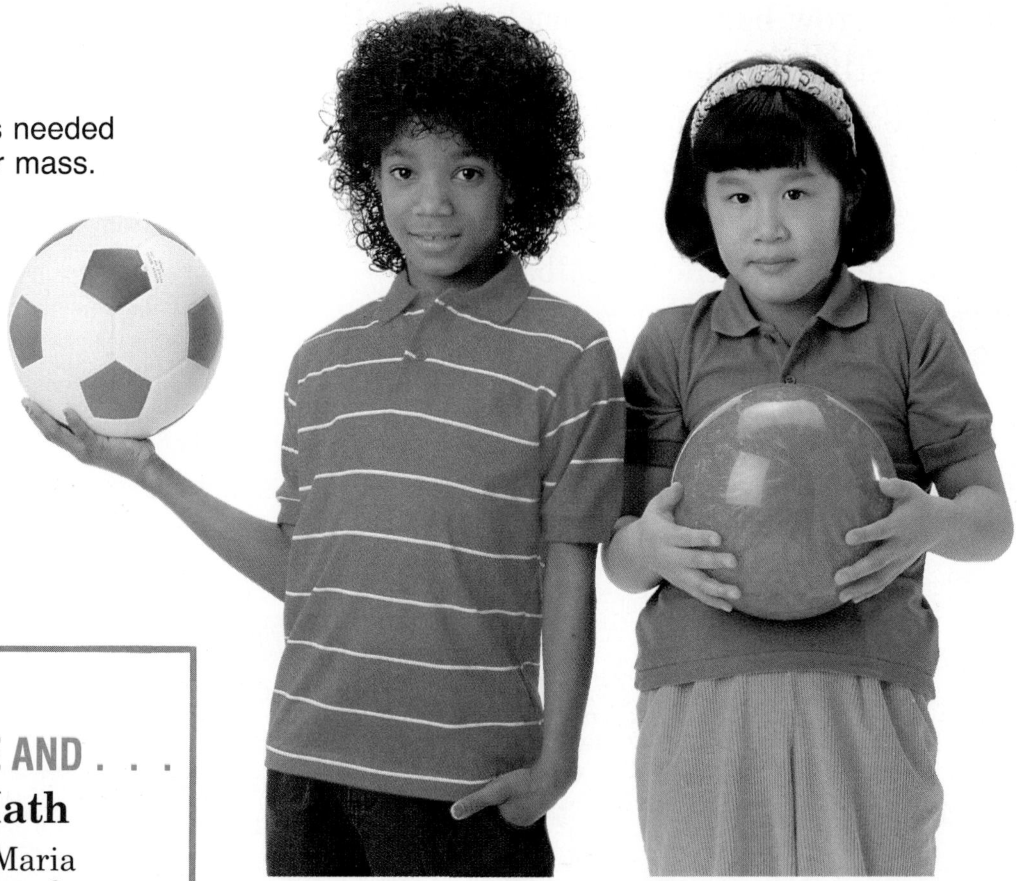

More force is needed to lift a larger mass.

SCIENCE AND . . .
Math

Lance and Maria carried boxes of supplies. Lance's box had a mass of 73 kg. Maria's had a mass of 39 kg. What was the mass of both boxes?
A. 112 kg.
B. 34 kg.
C. 102 kg.
D. 44 kg.

Lesson Summary

- Force is needed to move objects.
- The greater an object's mass, the more force is needed to move the object.

Lesson Review

1. What is force?

★2. Will more force be needed to push you or your teacher on a swing? Why?

How do you measure force?

What you need

cardboard strip
long rubber band
masking tape
30 cm string
3 paper clips
5 small objects
pencil and paper

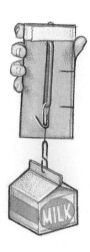

What to do

1. Make a "Puller Pal" like the one shown.
2. Make a pencil mark on the cardboard to show where the rubber band ends.
3. Hook an object to your Puller Pal. Lift the object.
4. Make a pencil mark on the cardboard to show how far the rubber band stretches. Write the name of the object by the mark.
5. Repeat steps 3 and 4 with all of the objects.

What did you learn?

1. Which object took the most force to lift? How do you know?
2. Which object took the least force?

Using what you learned

1. Suppose you had to lift two of the same kind of pens at once. Predict how much force you would need. Test your prediction.
2. Do you think more force is needed to pull a small book across a table or lift it? Use the Puller Pal to find out.

Gravity and Friction

LESSON 2 GOALS
You will learn
● that there is a pulling force between objects.
● that friction slows moving objects.
● that physical properties affect friction.

What is gravity?

Have you ever noticed that, no matter how high you jump, you always come back down? Or have you noticed that, no matter how high in the air you throw a ball, that ball always comes back down? There's a reason for that. Earth pulls on objects. This pull brings you back to Earth when you jump into the air. The attraction or pulling force between objects is called **gravity** (GRAV ut ee). Gravity is a property of all matter. The pull of gravity is greatest when two objects are close together. As the two objects get farther apart, the pulling force on each object becomes less.

Would You Believe?

At Earth's center, a person would be weightless because an equal amount of mass would pull him from all directions.

74

Friction

Friction (FRIHK shun) is the force that slows down or stops objects in motion. Imagine that you are riding a bike on level ground. If you stop pedaling, think about what happens. Friction between your bike tires and the ground slows you. Now imagine the same bike ride, but this time use the brakes. Think about what happens now. The friction that slows you this time is friction between your bike tires and the brake pads.

Friction happens whenever one object moves over another. The amount of friction depends on the kind of surfaces that touch each other. There is more friction when an object moves over a rough surface than when it moves over a smooth surface. For example, you are able to ride a sled very fast down a hill covered with snow. You could not ride a sled as easily on a grassy hill. Because the grass is not as smooth as snow, there is more friction.

What is friction?

SCIENCE AND . . .
Reading

Why is it safer to wear shoes with rough rubber soles than smooth leather soles on a wet, slippery day?
A. Rubber doesn't get wet.
B. Rubber has more friction.
C. Rubber costs more.

Friction is less on a smooth surface.

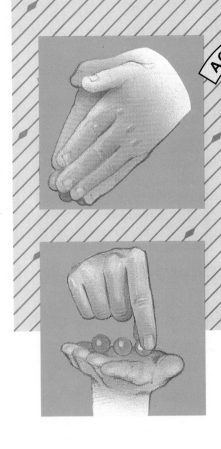

You Can...

Reduce Friction

Quickly rub your hands together about 20 times. How do they feel? Put several marbles in your hands and rub them together again. Do they feel as warm? Try it again, but first put a little liquid soap on your hands. How warm do they feel now? How else might you reduce friction?

Lesson Summary

- The attraction or pulling force between two objects is called gravity.
- Friction causes moving objects to slow down or stop.
- Contact between rough objects causes more friction than contact between smooth objects.

Lesson Review

1. Why do raindrops fall toward Earth?
★2. How would getting water or oil on your bike tires affect the brakes?

How can you change friction?

What you need

Puller Pal
chalkboard eraser
string
smooth table
sandpaper
dish towel
pencil and paper
metric ruler

What to do

1. Attach the Puller Pal to the eraser with a string.
2. Put the eraser on the table and hold the Puller Pal so the string is tight. Mark where the rubber band ends.
3. Slowly pull the eraser on the table top. Mark how far the rubber band stretches. Record this on a chart.
4. Repeat step 3, use a piece of sandpaper on the table.
5. Repeat step 3 again, putting a towel on the table.

What did you learn?

1. Which surface made the most friction? How do you know?
2. How did the sandpaper affect friction?

Using what you learned

1. What kind of surface would be the best to use with a skateboard?
2. Why can't you get rid of all friction?
3. How could you make more friction? Why would more friction be useful?

Work and Energy

LESSON 3 GOALS
You will learn
● that work is done when a force moves an object.
● that energy is used when work is done.
● that there are different sources of energy.

Did you know you are doing work even when you're playing a game? Scientists say that **work** is done when a force moves an object. Is work being done in the picture on this page? How do you know?

To find the amount of work done on an object, you need to know two things. You must know how much force is needed to move the object. You must also know how far the object is moved. That is, the amount of work done depends on both force and distance. More work was done when the wheelbarrow full of bricks was pushed than when the wheelbarrow full of branches was pushed. More work is also done if you push the wheelbarrow five meters instead of three meters.

Remember that an object must be moved for work to be done on the object. You may push with all your might on a stalled car. However, if you don't move the car, you haven't done work on the car.

Look at the picture below of the children playing a game of tug-of-war. As long as one team is able to pull the other team, you know that work is being done. However, if the teams are even in strength and neither team could move the other, no work is done. Why?

People need fuel.

What is energy?

Each time a force moves an object, such as the wheelbarrow or the teams, work is done. When work is done, energy (EN ur jee) is used. **Energy** is the ability to do work. The more work you do, the more energy you use.

To do work, people need a source of energy. People get energy from the food they eat.

Machines also need a source of energy. But machines can't eat food. What do machines use for energy? Sometimes forces in nature supply this energy. Falling water in a stream, for example, may turn a paddlewheel that turns a stone that grinds grain into flour.

Machines need fuel.

Most of the energy that runs machines is supplied by fuel or electricity. Gasoline supplies the energy needed to run the engines of cars. Electricity runs machines such as computers.

Whenever work is done by a machine or by a person, energy is needed. The more work you do, the more energy you use.

Lesson Summary

- The amount of work done depends on both force and distance.
- The more work you do, the more energy you use.
- Food and fuel are two sources of energy.

Lesson Review

1. When is work done on an object?
2. What is energy?
★3. Is work being done when you push on a door that won't open? Why or why not?

Choosing Good Wheels

Most skateboard wheels are made of polyurethane (pahlee YUR uh thayne). Polyurethane is a special plastic that has gas bubbled into it. Some wheels are better than others. How can you choose good wheels?

Some skateboard wheels are made quickly by machines. Hundreds can be made in an hour, so these wheels don't cost too much. A needle on a machine squirts polyurethane into molds. These wheels are not very hard, and there is too much friction to roll fast. You can tell when wheels are made this way by looking for a small hole on the surface where the needle was taken out.

The best wheels are made in polished steel or glass molds. Hot polyurethane is poured into the mold. The polyurethane is then baked in an oven to make it harder. Making these wheels takes about two weeks. That's why these wheels cost more.

Which wheels are best? Look for hard, smooth wheels that are colored evenly and don't have air bubbles.

Science and Technology

Summary

Lesson 1
- Force is needed to move objects.
- The amount of force needed to move an object depends on the object's mass.

Lesson 2
- Gravity is the pulling force between objects.
- Friction causes moving objects to slow down or stop.

- Rough surfaces cause more friction than smooth surfaces.

Lesson 3
- Work is done when a force moves an object.
- Energy is the ability to do work.
- Energy comes from many different sources.

Science Words

Fill in the blank with the correct word or words from the list.

**force   friction   energy
gravity   work**

1. When a force moves an object you have done ____.
2. The pulling force between objects is called ____.
3. ____ is the ability to do work.
4. A force that slows down moving objects is called ____.
5. A push or a pull is a(n) ____.

Questions

Recalling Ideas

Correctly complete each of the following sentences.

1. A ball falls when it is thrown because of
   (a) pressure. (c) friction.
   (b) gravity.   (d) air.

2. You may move an object when you use
   (a) air.   (c) mass.
   (b) friction. (d) force.

3. The force needed to lift an object depends on the object's
   (a) mass.   (c) friction.
   (b) energy.   (d) shape.

4. Work is being done when you are
   (a) reading. (c) holding a chair.
   (b) sitting.   (d) lifting a pencil.

5. If you push on an object but don't move it, you have
   (a) a large mass.
   (b) felt gravity.
   (c) not done work.
   (d) done work.

6. The amount of work done on an object depends on
   (a) force and distance.
   (b) distance and gravity.
   (c) force and friction.
   (d) mass and force.

Understanding Ideas

Answer the following questions using complete sentences.

1. Which will take more force to lift, (a) a wooden block the size of a chalkboard eraser or (b) a wooden block the size of a shoe box? Why?

2. Why are different amounts of force needed to move different objects?

3. Why is it hard for a car to stop on ice?

Thinking Critically

Think about what you have learned in this chapter. Answer the following questions using complete sentences.

1. You and a friend each pull a wagon up a hill. Both wagons are the same except yours is filled with books. Who does more work? Why?

2. Why are most playground slides made with smooth surfaces?

85

Machines

It is not easy to push a full grocery cart through the store. But think how much more difficult it would be to move those groceries without a cart to help you.

Have You Ever...

Moved a Load of Books?

Find a small box about the size of a lunchbox. Predict how many books you could put in the box and pull with a thread. Record your prediction, then experiment. How many books can you pull before the thread breaks? Now put the box into a toy truck or wagon. Predict the number of books you can pull. Will the number be the same, more, or less than your first prediction? Try it and see.

Simple Machines, Lever

LESSON 1 GOALS
You will learn
● why simple machines are important.
● why a lever is a simple machine.
● that not all levers are the same.

Jenny found a big rock in the middle of the bike path around the lake. "That could be dangerous," she said to her friend Erich. "Someone could have an accident. Let's move the rock off the path." But the rock was too heavy for Jenny and Erich to lift. They could barely push it.

Then Erich saw a long board and had an idea. "Here, Jenny," he said, "help me lift just one edge of the rock so we can slide the end of this board under it. There. Now we must push this log under the board close to the rock. Now I'll just push down hard on the other end of the board and see what happens!"

Wedge

Lever

Screw

Inclined plane

Wheel and axle

Pulley

Sure enough, the heavy rock rolled away when Erich pushed down on the board. The board and the log made a simple machine. People can use many kinds of machines to do work. A machine with only a few or even no moving parts is called a **simple machine.** Simple machines can be used to make work seem easier to do. They can change the amount of force needed to do work. They can also change the direction of the force. However, machines do not decrease the amount of work that is done. The pictures on this page show the six kinds of simple machines.

Lever

What should you remember about levers?

Jenny and Erich made a lever. A **lever** is a simple machine that is used to move objects. It is important to remember three things about levers. The object to be moved by a lever is called the load. The point where a lever rocks back and forth is called a fulcrum (FUL krum). The push or pull that moves a lever is the force. Find the load, fulcrum, and force on the lever that Jenny and Erich made.

Levers can also be used to change the direction of the force needed to lift an object. Think about a seesaw. When you push down on one end, the person on the other end goes up.

A hammer as a lever

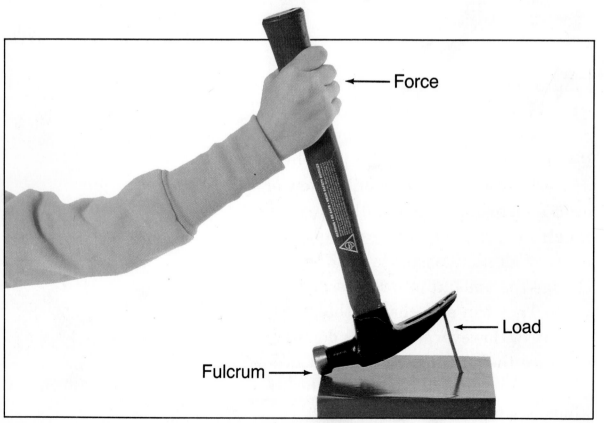

90

Levers can also be used to change the amount of force. Think about the seesaw again. Elena, the little girl in the top picture, wants to play on the seesaw with her older sister. She is too little to lift her older sister when the fulcrum is in the middle. When the fulcrum is moved closer to her older sister, as in the picture on the left, then Elena is able to lift her sister.

Look at the bottom picture. Elena's younger brother wants to ride on the seesaw. Elena is now the heavier one. Therefore, she must move the fulcrum closer to herself. Elena has discovered that the amount of force needed to lift a load depends on where the fulcrum is.

Load

Force

Fulcrum

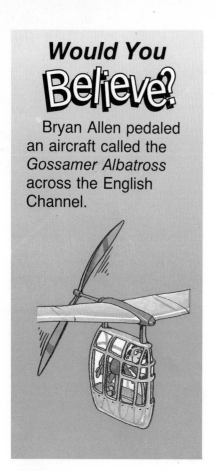
Jenny and Erich pushed the log close to the rock. With the fulcrum closer to the load, less force was needed to lift the load. What would have happened if they had not pushed it close to the rock?

Lesson Summary

- Simple machines can be used to change the amount of force needed to do work or to change the direction of a force.
- A simple machine has few or no moving parts and makes work seem easier to do.
- The position of the fulcrum is not the same on all levers.

Lesson Review

1. What is a simple machine?
2. What are the three parts of a lever?
★3. How does changing the position of the fulcrum on a lever change the amount of force needed?

Using a lever

How do levers work?

What you need

3 pencils
2 small paper cups
masking tape
metric ruler
clay
8 metal washers
pencil and paper

What to do

1. Tape a paper cup to each end of the ruler. Tape the pencils together as shown. Put them under the middle of the ruler.
2. Put a small clay ball in one of the cups.
3. Add washers one at a time to the other cup until the clay ball is lifted.
4. Record how many washers it took to lift the ball of clay.
5. Move the fulcrum and try again.

What did you learn?

1. What simple machine did you make?
2. What was the force?
3. What was the load?
4. How many washers lifted the load?

Using what you learned

1. You want to balance a 20-g box and a 10-g box on your ruler. Where should you put the pencils?
2. Why is it easier to pry open a can of paint using a long screwdriver rather than a short one?

93

Inclined Plane, Wedge, and Screw

LESSON 2 GOALS
You will learn
● that an inclined plane is a simple machine used to move objects.
● that a wedge has two important uses.
● that a screw is a type of inclined plane.

What is an inclined plane?

When you are riding your bike to the top of a hill, do you like to take the steepest path? Probably not, unless you are in a big hurry. You know that it means hard riding to take the steepest path. If you want to use less force, you take a longer path that isn't so steep.

A path going to the top of a hill is an example of an inclined plane. An **inclined plane** is a simple machine used to move objects to a higher or lower place. In the picture, both inclined planes reach the same high point. But one inclined plane is longer than the other. Because this inclined plane is not as steep, less force is needed to get to the top.

A **wedge** (WEJ) is a simple machine made of two inclined planes. Knife blades, chisels, pins, and the blade of a hatchet or ax are all examples of wedges. Work is done when the wedge presses against two objects. A wedge can be used to push objects apart. Logs are split by using axes and hatchets. The blade of the hatchet or ax is forced into the log. It pushes the pieces of log apart.

A **screw** is an inclined plane wrapped around a post. Screws, drill bits, and other objects commonly found in your home make use of the inclined plane. Have you ever used a screw to push two objects together? Have you ever seen a drill bit push some material out of the way?

Try making a screw by cutting an inclined plane out of paper. Wrap this paper around a cardboard tube. The edges of the paper are like the ridges of a screw.

How is a wedge useful?

Inclined plane around a post

Wedge

95

Suppose you had to pull a heavy load to the top of a hill. One path is very steep and goes straight up. The other path goes around and around the hill before reaching the top. Which path would you take with your heavy load? Why?

Lesson Summary

- An inclined plane is a simple machine used to move objects to higher or lower places.
- A wedge is a simple machine used to raise objects or to push them apart.
- A screw is an inclined plane wrapped around a post.

Lesson Review

1. Name two examples of inclined planes.
2. Tell how a screw and a wedge are like inclined planes.
★3. What simple machine is used to attach a hose to a faucet?

How do inclined planes make work easier?

What you need

4 books
Puller Pal
metric ruler
milk carton
8 marbles
ramp (board)
pencil and paper

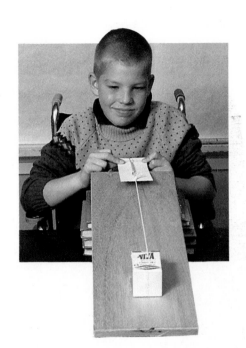

What to do

1. Pile 4 books on top of each other.
2. Put 8 marbles into the milk carton.
3. Lift the milk carton with the Puller Pal until the bottom of the carton is even with the top book.
4. Measure how far the rubber band stretches.
5. Set up the ramp, milk carton, and Puller Pal as shown.
6. Pull the carton up the ramp. Mark how far the rubber band stretches.

What did you learn?

1. Which way took more force to move the carton?
2. Which way took a longer distance?

Using what you learned

1. Find out what happens to the force needed if the ramp is made steeper.
2. Why are roads built around mountains instead of straight up the sides?

97

Wheel and Axle, Pulley

Wheels make loads easier to move. A **wheel and axle** is a simple machine with a wheel that turns a post. The post is called an axle. Wheels and axles are seen on cars, trains, trucks, and bicycles. Look at the picture of the doorknob and axle. The doorknob is the wheel that turns the axle. The distance around the doorknob is greater than the distance around the axle. Therefore, less force is needed to turn the wheel than to turn the axle.

Wheel and axle

98

Fixed pulley

Pulley

A pulley is a simple machine that changes the direction or amount of a force. A **pulley** is a wheel on a post with a rope around the wheel. A pulley may be fixed or movable. Each part of the rope that is wrapped around the pulley supports a part of the load. One fixed pulley is shown in the top drawing. A fixed pulley can make work seem easier to do by changing the direction of the force. This type of pulley is used to raise a flag on a flagpole. You pull down on the rope. As you pull down, the flag that is attached to the other side of the rope moves up the pole.

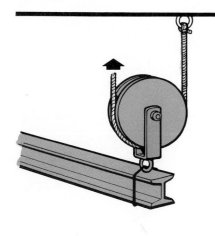

A movable pulley is shown in the drawing on this page. It is helpful in a different way. Using a movable pulley can decrease the force needed to lift a load. The force can be cut in half if one movable pulley is used to lift the load.

Using less force to lift a load makes the job seem easier. Pulleys and wheels and axles, like the other simple machines you have learned about in this chapter, make our jobs seem easier.

Lesson Summary

- A wheel and axle is a simple machine with a wheel that turns a post.
- A pulley is a simple machine that changes the direction or amount of force.

Lesson Review

1. Why is it easier to pull a cart with wheels than a cart with no wheels?
★2. Give examples of how a pulley can change the direction of a force.

Compound Machines

LESSON 4 GOALS
You will learn
● the difference between simple and compound machines.
● that most machines are compound machines.
● that people use compound machines for many reasons.

If you were asked to make a list of machines often found in kitchens, you might start with a stove and a refrigerator. But would you think to list a simple can opener? You should. A can opener is a machine. In fact, it is a compound machine. Most machines are compound machines. A **compound machine** is a machine made of two or more simple machines.

In a compound machine the simple machines are connected. The work each simple machine does is combined to do the job of the compound machine. For example, a can opener has three simple machines. The blade of the opener is a wedge. A lever forces the blade into the can. The force used to open the can is applied to a wheel and axle.

Compound machine

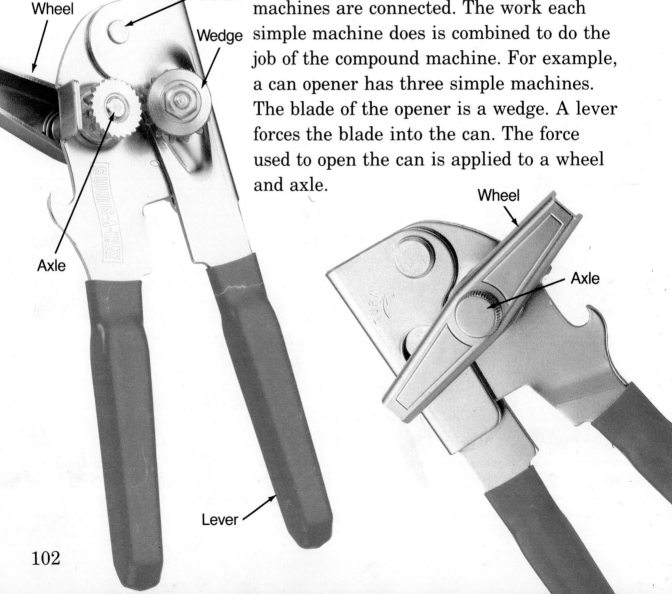

Wheel

Fulcrum

Wedge

Axle

Lever

Wheel

Axle

102

You Can...

Invent a Machine

Think about the simple machines you have learned about. Now, invent a machine using two or more simple machines. First, draw a picture of your machine. Label the simple machines in your drawing. Then, build a model of your machine. Display it in class. Tell your classmates how it works and what it does.

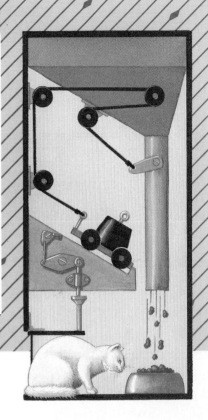

People Use Machines

How did you get to school today? If you rode in a bus or car or on your bicycle, you used a compound machine. People can use compound machines to move themselves or objects from place to place. Machines that carry people and objects are kinds of transportation. Bicycles, trucks, trains, boats, and planes are compound machines that are kinds of transportation.

People use machines for other reasons, too. Machines are useful in factories. People also use machines in growing food. Machines can do some work more quickly than people can. Machines also do work that is dangerous or harmful to people.

How would you try to open a can of soup if you didn't have a can opener? It would be very difficult and dangerous. A can opener is just one example of how machines can make our lives easier.

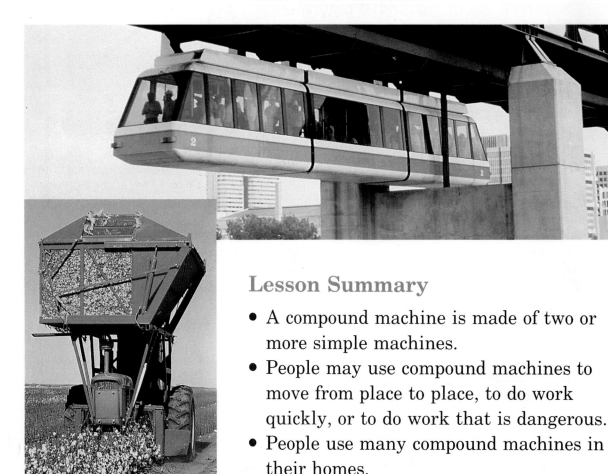

Compound machines

Lesson Summary

- A compound machine is made of two or more simple machines.
- People may use compound machines to move from place to place, to do work quickly, or to do work that is dangerous.
- People use many compound machines in their homes.

Lesson Review

1. What is the difference between a simple and a compound machine?
2. Name two compound machines found in the home.
★3. Why would a compound machine sometimes be more useful than a simple machine?

Use Application Activity on pages 347, 348.

A Bicycle Tester

Joseph Pérex is a bicycle racer who also test-rides bicycles. Some tests require that Joseph lie on his back to pedal the bikes. These bikes are designed for speed. Another bike that Joseph has been testing is an enclosed bike. A canopy, or cover, is placed over the frame and the rider. Scientists hope to discover a canopy that will lower wind resistance without adding much weight.

Joseph enjoys testing bicycles, but he also wants to compete in the Olympics some day. After the Olympics, Joseph hopes to test pedal-powered aircraft and boats.

Improvements from testing cars, aircraft, and other experimental products often find their way to the general public. The same is true with bicycle improvements. In a few years, your new bike may look like one Joseph has been testing.

Career

105

Summary

Lesson 1
- Simple machines change the amount or direction of force.
- Simple machines have few or no moving parts.

Lesson 2
- Inclined planes are used to move objects.
- Inclined planes, wedges, and screws are similar.

Lesson 3
- A wheel and axle is a wheel that turns a post.
- A pulley changes the direction or amount of a force.

Lesson 4
- Compound machines contain two or more simple machines.
- Most machines are compound machines.

Science Words

Fill in the blank with the correct word or words from the list.

simple machine	screw
wheel and axle	lever
inclined plane	pulley
compound machine	wedge

1. A machine made of two or more simple machines is called a(n) ____ .
2. A doorknob is an example of a(n) ____ .
3. An inclined plane wrapped around a post is a(n) ____ .
4. A ramp is a(n) ____ .
5. A knife blade is an example of a(n) ____ .
6. A machine with few or no moving parts is a(n) ____ .
7. A simple machine with a rope and a wheel is a(n) ____ .
8. A seesaw is an example of a(n) ____ .

Questions

Recalling Ideas

Correctly complete each of the following sentences.

1. The simple machine formed from two inclined planes is a
   (a) wedge. (c) lever.
   (b) screw. (d) wheel and axle.
2. A can opener is a compound machine that contains a wedge, lever, and
   (a) fixed pulley.
   (b) inclined plane.
   (c) movable pulley.
   (d) wheel and axle.
3. A doorknob is a
   (a) wedge. (c) wheel and axle.
   (b) screw. (d) pulley.
4. Simple machines can change the direction or the amount of
   (a) work. (c) energy.
   (b) force. (d) mass.

Understanding Ideas

Answer the following questions using complete sentences.

1. Give two reasons why a pulley is used to lift an object.
2. How does work seem easier to do when an inclined plane is used?

Thinking Critically

Think about what you have learned in this chapter. Answer the following questions using complete sentences.

1. Why are machines often used to paint cars in factories?
2. How do you change the position of the fulcrum on a lever in order to move a heavier load?

Checking for Understanding

Write a short answer for each question or statement.

1. What are scientific methods, and how can they be used to help you?
2. Name five properties that describe objects.
3. Why is more force used to lift a bowling ball than a soccer ball?
4. Compare compound machines and simple machines.
5. What units are used to measure the mass of an object?
6. In what way are solids and liquids the same?
7. What is the difference between evaporation and condensation?
8. What is the difference between a mixture and a compound?
9. If you push on a big box but it doesn't move, why haven't you done any work?
10. Describe the difference between work and energy.
11. How are a wedge and a screw alike? different?
12. Name several uses for a wheel and axle.
13. How are compound machines used outside the home?

Recalling Activities

Write a short paragraph for each question or statement.

1. How fast will sugar dissolve?
2. How can you find the best soap?
3. How do you measure mass?
4. Is it a solid or a liquid?
5. How can you make a dime dance?
6. How does water change?
7. How do you measure force?
8. How can you change friction?
9. How do levers work?
10. How do inclined planes make work easier?

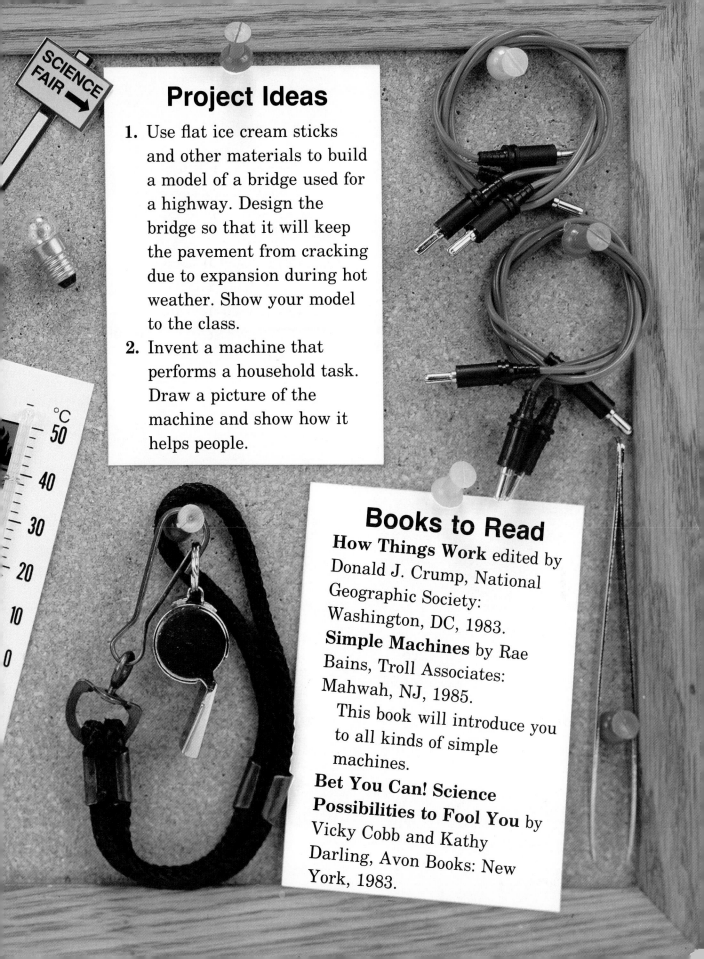

Project Ideas

1. Use flat ice cream sticks and other materials to build a model of a bridge used for a highway. Design the bridge so that it will keep the pavement from cracking due to expansion during hot weather. Show your model to the class.

2. Invent a machine that performs a household task. Draw a picture of the machine and show how it helps people.

Books to Read

How Things Work edited by Donald J. Crump, National Geographic Society: Washington, DC, 1983.

Simple Machines by Rae Bains, Troll Associates: Mahwah, NJ, 1985.

This book will introduce you to all kinds of simple machines.

Bet You Can! Science Possibilities to Fool You by Vicky Cobb and Kathy Darling, Avon Books: New York, 1983.

SCIENCE FAIR →

Earth Science

The rain to the wind said,
"You push and I'll pelt."
They so smote the garden bed
That the flowers actually knelt,
And lay lodged—though not dead.
I know how the flowers felt.

"Lodged"
Robert Frost

CHAPTER 6

Rocks

Along the highway, you may have seen places where the rock has been cut so a road can go through. Sometimes you can see patterns in the rock. Patterns like the one in the picture show how many layers of sand, shells, or plants helped form the rock.

ACTIVITY

Have You Ever...

Made Layers?

Pour 236 mL of red gelatin into a loaf pan. Cool in the refrigerator until firm. Add 236 mL of yellow gelatin and cool until firm. Slice bananas and cover the yellow gelatin. Pour on 236 mL of green gelatin and cool until firm. Cut a slice of gelatin. How is your dessert like the picture on page 112?

Rocks and Earth's Layers

LESSON 1 GOALS

You will learn
● that rocks are made of minerals.
● that rocks have different properties.
● that Earth has layers.

Carla likes to collect rocks. She often wonders how the rocks formed. Her favorite rocks are shown in the picture on this page. Each rock has different properties. How would you describe each rock?

Carla's favorite rocks

What Are Rocks?

A gelatin salad is somewhat like a rock. The salad is a mixture of gelatin and different fruit. In the picture of gelatin salad on this page, you can see the different parts mixed together. You might see pieces of peach, pear, or grape. The pieces are different colors, sizes, and shapes. How many different parts of the salad mixture do you see?

114

Rocks are also mixtures of different things. You can often see parts of the mixture. Look at the rock pictured on this page. What different colors do you see? Each different color is a different part of the rock.

The different parts that make a rock are called minerals (MIHN uh rulz). A **mineral** is a solid found in nature. Minerals are made of chemicals. They are not living, and their inside structures are crystals.

Mica

Quartz

Granite

Feldspar

It is fun to look at some rocks that are mixtures of different minerals. Just as minerals have different properties, rocks also have different properties. Some rocks are made of many different minerals and are colorful. Other rocks are made of just one mineral and are plain. Some rocks are smooth, and others are rough. Some rocks are very hard, and others are soft.

Where Are Rocks Found?

Earth has layers like a peach. When you slice a peach, you can see its layers. A thin skin is all around the outside. A thick layer is in the middle. A seed is in the center. Scientists cannot slice Earth, of course. But scientists know that Earth has layers, too. Look at the peach and Earth in the picture on this page. Compare them.

The outside layer of Earth is called the **crust.** Mountains, valleys, and ocean floors are all part of Earth's crust. Most of the crust is solid rock. The small rocks you find on the ground come from larger rocks of the crust. Some areas of the crust are covered with soil.

How are a peach and Earth similar?

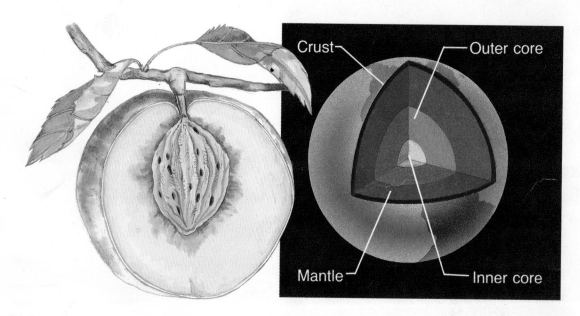

The layers of a peach are like Earth's.

116

The crust is thin like the skin of a peach. Earth's crust, however, is not even in thickness. It is thin in some places and thick in others. Ocean-floor crust is thinner than the crust under land areas. The crust of the ocean floor is about 5 kilometers thick. The crust is about 35 kilometers thick under most land areas. It is even thicker under mountains.

Earth's crust is not even in thickness.

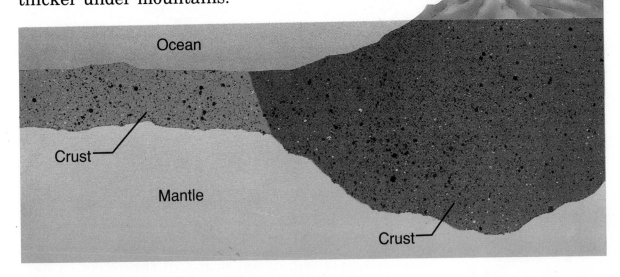

Land area

Ocean

Crust

Mantle

Crust

Other rock beneath the crust make up the **mantle** (MANT ul). The mantle is Earth's middle layer. It can be compared to the middle part of the peach, the part that you eat. Mantle rocks are different from rocks in the crust. Mantle rocks are more tightly packed. Some are partly melted.

Like a peach, Earth also has a center section. The **core** is the hottest and innermost part of Earth. It has two parts. The outer core is liquid. The inner core is solid. Both parts of the core are very hot and made mostly of iron.

How are mantle rocks different from rocks in Earth's crust?

Carla wondered if any of the rocks in her collection had come from Earth's mantle. She decided to read some more about rocks.

Lesson Summary

- Rocks are made of one or more minerals.
- Rocks may be smooth or rough, colorful or plain.
- The crust, mantle, and core are layers of Earth.

Lesson Review

1. What is a mineral?
★2. How are Earth's layers like a peach?

Use Application Activity on pages 351, 352.

How can sediments make layers?

What you need

clear plastic jar with lid
soil mixture
newspaper
hand lens
water
crayons
pencil and paper

What to do

1. Use the hand lens to observe the soil mixture, and write your observations on a chart. Fill 1/3 of the jar with this soil.
2. Add water until the jar is almost full. Tightly screw on the lid.
3. Shake the jar up and down 10 times.
4. Put the jar on a table and wait 10 minutes. Use the hand lens to observe what happens. Draw what you see and fill in your chart.

What did you learn?

1. How did the soil mixture look at first?
2. What happened after you shook the jar?
3. In what order did the particles settle?

Using what you learned

1. What are the layers of particles called?
2. Where can you find layers like this outside?
3. How might these layers be changed into rock?

How Rocks Form

LESSON 2 GOALS
You will learn
● that there are three types of rocks.
● how some kinds of rock form.
● that changes take place in rocks as part of the rock cycle.

Carla looked closely at one of the rocks from her rock collection. It was entirely black and seemed very light for its size. It seemed to be made of millions of tiny bubbles. How had it been formed?

Some rocks form from melted Earth material. Hot liquid material that forms inside Earth is called **magma** (MAG muh). Magma moves around inside Earth, and in some places it comes near the surface.

Sometimes magma flows onto Earth's surface. A magma flow often takes place at a volcano. When magma reaches Earth's surface, it is called **lava** (LAHV uh).

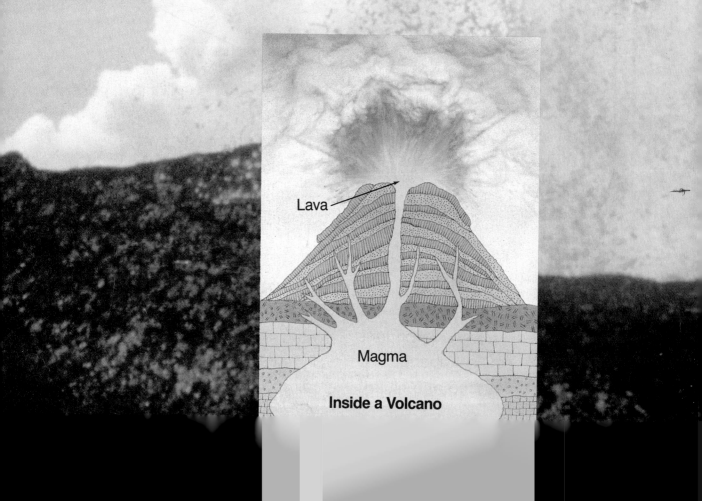

Lava

Magma

Inside a Volcano

A rock that forms from cooled magma or lava is called an **igneous** (IHG nee us) **rock.** Igneous rocks don't all look the same. Magma cools much more slowly than lava because it is still underground. The igneous rocks that form when magma cools slowly have large minerals. You can see the minerals without a hand lens.

Lava cools quickly because it is above the ground. Large minerals don't have time to form. Rocks formed from cooled lava have small mineral pieces. The mineral pieces may be so small you can't see them.

Carla looked again at her rock. She couldn't see any mineral pieces in it, so she decided it had been formed from cooled lava.

Rocks Formed From Sediments

Water, wind, and ice are constantly breaking large rocks into smaller rocks. Small rocks are breaking into even smaller pieces. These pieces are called sediments (SED uh munts). **Sediments** are pieces of Earth material. They are carried by wind, ice, and water. When the wind or water slows down or the ice melts, the sediments are dropped. After a period of time, the sediments become pressed together to form rock. A **sedimentary** (sed uh MENT uh ree) **rock** is a rock made of sediments that are pressed together.

What are sedimentary rocks made of?

Some sedimentary rocks are made when sediments pile up in a lake or ocean. Limestone is a sedimentary rock formed in this way. Some small sea animals use the mineral calcite in the water to make their shells. When they die, they fall to the ocean floor where they pile up. Over a very long time, these shells form layers and harden into rock. Sometimes the shells are big enough to see, and sometimes they are very tiny.

Sandstone

Limestone

Rocks Formed From Other Rocks

Deep inside Earth it is very hot, and the pressure is great. Rock that is buried deep inside Earth becomes hot and is under great pressure. Temperature and pressure can change rocks. A rock that has been changed by heat and pressure is a **metamorphic** (met uh MOR fihk) **rock.** Igneous and sedimentary rocks can become metamorphic rocks. Heat and pressure can also change one type of metamorphic rock into another type of metamorphic rock.

Metamorphic rocks can be grouped by the way they look. Some of them have stripes caused by great pressures within Earth. Other metamorphic rocks are not striped. Which metamorphic rock in the picture on this page is striped?

Carla looked at her rock collection. She found that she had several striped rocks. Proudly she added the word *metamorphic* to their labels.

124

ACTIVITY

You Can...
Study Rocks Made by People

Observe a piece of concrete with a hand lens. Draw what you see. Now observe a piece of asphalt and make a second drawing. Use resource materials to find out how concrete and asphalt are made. What kinds of natural rocks are these two most like? Why do you think this is so?

The Rock Cycle

A cycle is a set of changes that happen over and over again. Day and night make a cycle. Spring, summer, fall, and winter make a cycle, too. Can you think of other cycles?

Rocks go through a cycle, too. You have just learned the three different kinds of rocks and how they form. These rocks are all closely related. Over very long periods of time, rocks change. The cycle of change that sedimentary, igneous, and metamorphic rocks go through is called the **rock cycle.**

What is the rock cycle?

Look at the drawing of the rock cycle on this page. There is no beginning or end to the rock cycle. An igneous rock could be broken up by water, wind, and ice to form a sedimentary rock. It could also be heated and put under great pressure to become a metamorphic rock. A sedimentary rock can be melted to form an igneous rock, or it can be heated and put under great pressure to form a metamorphic rock. A metamorphic rock can be broken up by water, wind, and ice to form a sedimentary rock. It can also be melted to form an igneous rock.

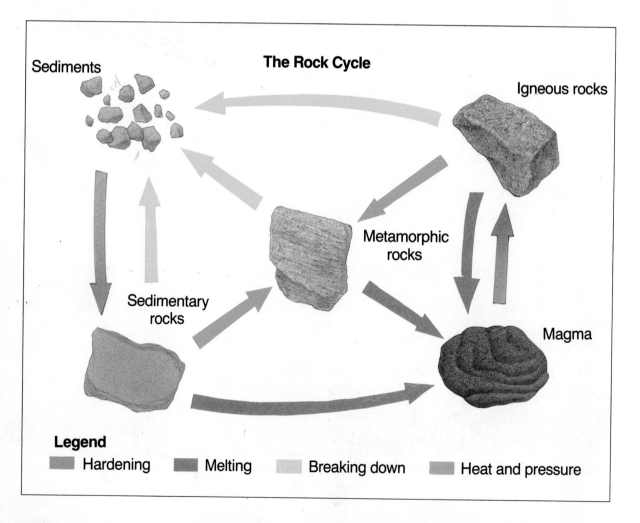

The Rock Cycle

Sediments

Igneous rocks

Metamorphic rocks

Sedimentary rocks

Magma

Legend

Hardening Melting Breaking down Heat and pressure

Carla said to herself, "That's really interesting. I've always thought of a rock as something that doesn't change. And that's true, when you compare the rock cycle with one that changes really fast, like day and night or the seasons. But now I'm finding out that everything changes. Some things change fast, and rocks change very, very slowly."

SCIENCE AND . . .
Math

At school, Mariko showed her rock collection in 7 rows of 8 rocks each. Alonzo showed his rocks in 9 rows of 6 rocks each. Who had more rocks? How many more?
A. Alonzo, 7 more
B. Mariko, 7 more
C. Alonzo, 2 more
D. Mariko, 2 more

Lesson Summary

- Igneous, sedimentary, and metamorphic are the three types of rocks found on Earth.
- Igneous, sedimentary, and metamorphic rocks are formed in different ways.
- Each type of rock is changed to a different type of rock as part of the rock cycle.

Lesson Review

1. Give two examples of a cycle.
2. What is lava?
★3. Describe how an igneous rock might be changed to a sedimentary rock.

How does sedimentary rock form?

What you need

paper cup
cementing solution
sand
hand lens
newspaper
pencil and paper

What to do

1. Fill the cup half full of sand. Pack the sand with your hand. Tell what the sand is like using a chart.
2. Slowly add cementing solution until all of the sand is wet.
3. Put the cup in a warm place until the sand dries completely.
4. Carefully tear away the paper cup.
5. Observe the "sandstone" with the hand lens. Write about what you see on your chart.

What did you learn?

1. How did the sand change?
2. How is your "rock" like sedimentary rock?

Using what you learned

1. If you found clam shells in sedimentary rock, what could you say about the place where the rock formed?
2. Why is your "sandstone" not a rock?

I WANT TO KNOW ABOUT...

A Rock Scientist

Peter Schwans is a scientist who studies and describes rocks. Peter studies sedimentary rock in Utah, a state that has plenty of rocks!

Peter spends every summer collecting rock samples. To begin a day's work, he drives a van over rough country high into the mountains. He uses a rock hammer to break off rock pieces and takes them back to the lab to study.

Peter also takes notes. He marks each day's work on a map that shows Earth's surface. He marks the kinds of rocks that are above and below the ones he has broken off. Peter uses his map to find out what this part of Utah was like long ago.

Peter has learned that Utah used to be much different. Millions of years ago, Utah was covered by a large sea that washed away the mountain ranges. This Earth material later formed the sedimentary rocks that Peter studies today.

Career

Summary

Lesson 1
- Rocks are made of one or more minerals.
- Rocks may be smooth or rough, colorful or plain, made of minerals or just one mineral.
- Earth's layers are the crust, mantle, and core.

Lesson 2
- Three types of rocks are igneous, sedimentary, and metamorphic.
- Igneous, sedimentary, and metamorphic rocks are formed in different ways.
- Rocks change through a process called the rock cycle.

Science Words

Fill in the blank with the correct word or words from the list.

mineral	lava
crust	igneous
mantle	sediments
core	sedimentary
magma	metamorphic
	rock cycle

1. Cooled magma forms ____ .
2. Earth's top layer is the ____ .

3. Sediments that are pressed together form ____ .
4. Earth's middle layer is the ____ .
5. The innermost part of Earth is the ____ .
6. A rock changed by heat and pressure is called ____ .
7. Solid matter found in nature that is not made by plants or animals is a(n) ____ .

130

Questions

Recalling Ideas

Correctly complete each of the following sentences.

1. Magma forms rocks with
   - (a) large minerals.
   - (b) small minerals.
   - (c) no minerals.
   - (d) only one mineral.
2. Rocks are mixtures of
   - (a) magma.
   - (c) minerals.
   - (b) gelatin.
   - (d) lava.
3. Most of Earth's crust is
   - (a) very hot.
   - (c) liquid.
   - (b) solid rock.
   - (d) partly melted.
4. Rocks formed from lava have
   - (a) large minerals.
   - (b) small minerals.
   - (c) medium minerals.
   - (d) large and small minerals.

Understanding Ideas

Answer the following questions using complete sentences.

1. How do sedimentary rocks form?
2. Tell about Earth's layers and the rocks in these layers.
3. Describe a metamorphic rock as it changes in the rock cycle.

Thinking Critically

Think about what you have learned in this chapter. Answer the following questions using complete sentences.

1. What could you do in order to decide whether a certain igneous rock formed near the surface of Earth or deeper inside Earth's crust?
2. If you found a rock that appeared to be made of smaller rocks and shells, what kind would it be and how would it have formed?

Nature Changes Rocks

You may have collected rocks at the beach. You may have looked for rocks in a river. Rocks you find near the water often feel smooth to the touch. How do you think moving water might change a rock's surface from rough to smooth?

Have You Ever...

Made Changes in Rocks?

Gather together two rocks and a piece of paper. Rub the rocks together over the paper for three minutes. Observe the paper. What do you see? What would eventually happen to the rocks if you continued to rub them together?

Weathering

LESSON 1 GOALS
You will learn
● that weathering is always taking place.
● that four forces in nature change rocks.

In the picture on this page, Leon is hunting for certain kinds of stones. He wants to throw the stones across the water and make them skip. He looks for stones that are flat and smooth with rounded edges. Leon wonders, "How do they get that way? Most rocks are rough. They have sharp edges. Where do the smooth stones come from?"

Water, wind, ice, and living things change rocks. The change often happens slowly. Over a long period of time, rocks are broken into smaller parts. The breaking down or wearing away of rock is called **weathering.** Weathering is always taking place.

What is weathering?

134

Water and Wind Change Rocks

Water changes rocks in different ways. Fast-moving water moves rocks downstream. As they move, the rocks bump into each other. Over a long time, the rocks wear down and become smooth and rounded. Leon's skipping stones have been worn down by moving water. Look at the picture of the rocks on this page. How has the river changed these rocks?

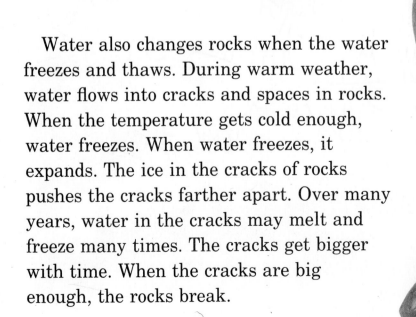

Water also changes rocks when the water freezes and thaws. During warm weather, water flows into cracks and spaces in rocks. When the temperature gets cold enough, water freezes. When water freezes, it expands. The ice in the cracks of rocks pushes the cracks farther apart. Over many years, water in the cracks may melt and freeze many times. The cracks get bigger with time. When the cracks are big enough, the rocks break.

Water can change rocks in yet another way. Rain and groundwater can soak into rocks. Some minerals in rocks dissolve in the water. The water carries away the minerals from the rocks. Holes are left where the minerals used to be.

There is another way ice can weather rocks. A **glacier** (GLAY shur) is a large mass of ice that moves. Frozen in the glacier are large rocks, sand, and soil. The rocks scratch the surfaces over which the glaciers move. The picture of the rock with long scratches shows a rock weathered by a glacier.

What is a glacier?

Glaciers weather rock.

Wind also weathers rocks. Strong winds pick up and carry dust and sand. These small particles scratch rocks, and the rocks slowly wear away. Sometimes windblown sediments weather rocks into strange shapes.

Wind weathers rock.

Plants break rocks.

Plants and Animals Change Rocks

Plants, too, can change rocks. Some plants grow in soil that has collected in the cracks of rocks. The plant roots push on the rocks as the plants grow. The rocks may break if the plants grow large enough. Strong tree roots can even break sidewalks and curbs. Look around your neighborhood. See if you can find places where plants are breaking sidewalks.

Some animals change rocks. Animals make places for weathering to happen. Some animals dig tunnels in the ground and loosen rocks and soil. Air and water can then move deeper into the ground.

People change rocks, too. People use machines to break rocks. People dig tunnels and build roads through rocks. People build houses or statues out of rocks. To get enough small rocks to use for buildings, workers break the rocks into small pieces. The pieces are then put together to make walls or to cover roofs. The people in the pictures on this page are changing rocks. How can you change rocks?

Lesson Summary

- Rocks are constantly worn away or broken down by weathering.
- Water, wind, ice, and living things change rocks.

Lesson Review

1. What is weathering?
2. Describe how plants can change rock.
★3. How can water change rock?

People change rocks.

How can water break rocks?

What you need

plastic film container with lid
water
masking tape
freezer
pencil and paper

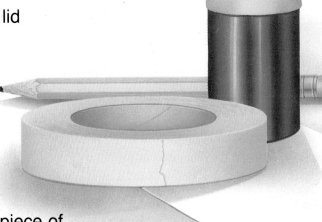

What to do

1. Write your name on a piece of tape. Place it on the film container.
2. Fill the container with water and snap the lid on tightly. Draw a picture of the container on your chart.
3. Place the container in a freezer for one day.
4. Remove the container and observe it. Draw the picture on your chart.

Container before freezing	Container after freezing

What did you learn?

1. How has the water changed?
2. What happened to the container?
3. What caused the change?

Using what you learned

1. Why isn't it safe to put glass bottles filled with liquid in a freezer?
2. Suppose water freezes in empty spaces in a rock. What might happen to the rock?

Soil and Erosion

When you pick up a handful of soil, you have weathered rock in your hand. Water, wind, ice, and living things break rocks into small pieces. Over time, weathering makes the pieces even smaller. The weathered rock becomes soil when it mixes with decayed plants and animals.

The kind of soil formed depends on the kind of weathered rock and the amount of decayed plants and animals. Clay-rich rocks will weather to form clay-rich soils. Soils rich in decayed plants and animals are good for growing crops. Spaces between small pieces of soil hold water, air, and nutrients needed by plants.

Would You Believe?

It takes 100 pounds of water to produce a single pound of food.

Top soil

Subsoil

Rock layer

You Can...

Study Soil Erosion

Place a mixture of damp mud, sand, gravel, and pebbles at the top of a stream table. Use 3 books to raise the top. Use a sprinkling bottle or watering can to make it rain on the mixture. Which particles move fastest and farthest down the slope? What size of soil particles on hills and in fields is most easily eroded by water?

Erosion

Water, wind, and ice weather rocks and also cause erosion (ih ROH zhun). **Erosion** is the movement of soil and rocks to new places. Hillsides erode when water from heavy rains carries away soil and loose rocks. When the water slows down, soil and rocks are dropped in other places.

Fast-moving water in rivers and streams also causes erosion. Rocks and soil from upstream are carried downstream.

Wind causes erosion in dry areas. Strong winds can pick up and carry away loose dirt and sand.

Erosion changes rocks.

Glaciers erode Earth's surface. As glaciers move, rocks and sediments become frozen in the ice and move along with the glacier. When the ice melts, rocks and sediments drop off along the edges of the glacier.

Glaciers, wind, rain, or rivers may have moved soil and rocks to your area. Over time, erosion moves soil from one place to another. Erosion and weathering are always taking place.

Lesson Summary

- Soil is made of pieces of rocks and plant and animal parts.
- Water, wind, and ice move soil and rocks to new places.

Lesson Review

1. Which soils are good for growing crops?
2. What is erosion?
★3. How does water cause erosion?

SCIENCE AND . . .
Reading

Choose the best summary of the **entire** chapter.
A. People use machines to change rocks.
B. Rocks can be changed into strange shapes.
C. Wind, water, and ice change rocks and cause erosion.

Use with Application Activity on pages 353, 354.

How do different soils compare?

What you need

3 soil samples
hand lens
3 paper cups
6 bean seeds
water
metric ruler
3 labels
pencil and paper

What to do

1. Use the hand lens to observe soils A, B, and C. Record how the soils look and feel.
2. Fill each paper cup with a different soil sample. Pack down the soils.
3. Label each cup A, B, or C to go with the soil samples.
4. Plant 2 seeds in each cup and place them by a window.
5. Add equal amounts of water to moisten the soil. Repeat this step as needed.
6. Measure and record plant growth on a chart after the first and second weeks.

What did you learn?

1. How do the soil colors and textures compare?
2. In which soil did the plants grow best?

Using what you learned

1. Which soil is best in a garden? Why?
2. Why should each cup of soil get equal amounts of water and light?

Summary

Lesson 1
- Rocks are constantly worn away or broken down.
- Water, wind, ice, and living things weather rocks.

Lesson 2
- Soil is pieces of rocks and decayed plants and animals.
- Water, wind, and ice move soil and rocks, causing erosion.

Science Words

Fill in the blank with the correct word or words from the list.

weathering

erosion   **glacier**

1. The movement of soil and rocks to new places is ___.
2. The breaking down of rocks is called ___.

Questions

Recalling Ideas

Correctly complete each of the following sentences.

1. Animals affect the weathering of Earth when
   (a) they sleep.
   (b) they drink water.
   (c) they dig tunnels.
   (d) they eat food.

2. Earth's rocks are
   (a) never changing.
   (b) always changing.
   (c) always large.
   (d) never broken.

3. Rocks may break when plants
   (a) decay.   (c) dig tunnels.
   (b) grow.   (d) dissolve.

4. Soils that are good for growing crops are rich in
   (a) clay.
   (b) sand.
   (c) clay and sand.
   (d) decayed plants and animals.

5. Wind causes erosion in
   (a) cold areas.   (c) dry areas.
   (b) warm areas. (d) wet areas.

6. Rocks with rounded edges were worn down by
   (a) being thrown.
   (b) moving water.
   (c) snow.
   (d) freezing water.

7. Ice in the cracks of rocks
   (a) smooths rocks.
   (b) melts rocks.
   (c) makes cracks larger.
   (d) makes cracks smaller.

Understanding Ideas

Answer the following questions using complete sentences.

1. How is soil formed?
2. How does water change rocks?
3. How can glaciers cause weathering and erosion?

Thinking Critically

Think about what you have learned in this chapter. Answer the following questions using complete sentences.

1. Why do you never really see the "same" rocks from one year to the next even though you live in the same area?
2. How do weathering and erosion affect the life of a farmer who grows crops?

145

Weather and Climate

Weather is a result of the condition of Earth's air. The air may be warm or cold, wet or dry. As the air condition changes, so does the weather.

Have You Ever...

Made Dew Drops?

One condition that changes our weather is the changing state of water in the air. Put some water into a pitcher. Record the temperature. Now add ice and stir the water. Keep adding ice and keep stirring the water until drops of water form on the outside of the pitcher. Then measure the temperature again. What is the temperature when the drops form? What caused the water drops to form? How does this help explain how dew is formed?

Evaporation and Condensation

LESSON 1 GOALS
You will learn
● that water changes from a liquid to a gas during evaporation.
● that two factors affect the speed of evaporation.
● that condensation may take place when water as a gas cools.

What is the atmosphere?

"It really got cold fast! I wish I had brought my jacket with me. But it was sunny and warm when I left, so how was I to know?" Does this sound like you? How many times can you remember needing a jacket or an umbrella that you hadn't brought? The weather can change quickly.

Weather changes take place in Earth's atmosphere (AT muh sfihr). The **atmosphere** is all the air around Earth.

Evaporation

Remember from Lesson 2 in Chapter 3 that evaporation is the change of matter from a liquid to a gas. When water is the matter that is evaporating, the gas formed is called **water vapor.** When water vapor evaporates from oceans, lakes, and rivers, it enters the air. Living plants and animals also give off water vapor.

Water changes to water vapor.

We can't see water vapor. However, after a storm we can see that puddles grow smaller and finally disappear. How does the drying of puddles show that water vapor forms?

Water can evaporate only where it meets the air. If a large surface meets the air, a lot of water can evaporate. If the surface meeting the air is small, not much water can evaporate.

How does surface area affect evaporation?

Water evaporates faster from one container.

Look at the two containers in the picture on this page. Both hold the same amount of water. Which one has a larger surface meeting the air? From which container will water evaporate faster?

Warm air speeds evaporation. In Lesson 3 in Chapter 2, you learned that particles of liquids bump into each other. When a liquid is heated, the particles move faster. They bump each other harder then. Some particles are bumped away from the surface of the liquid. These particles become a gas.

Suppose you hung wet clothes on a clothesline to dry. Would the clothes dry faster on a cool day or on a warm day? Wet clothes will dry faster if the weather is warm, since warm air speeds evaporation.

Moving air speeds evaporation, too. Have you ever washed your hands and then discovered that there were no towels? How did you dry your hands?

Wet hair and clothes dry faster on windy days. On a warm, dry day, where would clothes dry faster—inside a closed garage or out in the windy backyard? Clothes dry faster in the wind, since moving air speeds evaporation. How is a clothes dryer like a warm, dry, windy day?

Condensation

Water vapor is a gas, but it can change back to a liquid. In Lesson 2 in Chapter 3, you learned that the change of matter from a gas to a liquid is called condensation. Condensation changes water vapor to liquid water. For water vapor to condense to a liquid, it must become cooler. This cooling and condensation can take place in the air or on the ground.

When water vapor condenses on dust particles in the atmosphere, clouds form. Water vapor may also condense on objects on the ground. **Dew** is a form of condensation. When air cools at night, droplets of water called dew may form on cars and blades of grass.

When the air cools to below 0°C, water vapor may change to ice without first becoming dew. In that case, the water vapor condenses to form **frost.** In what season would you see frost on cars and blades of grass? Why should you wear a jacket or coat if you see frost?

Lesson Summary

- Evaporation is the change of matter from a liquid to a gas.
- Air temperature and air speed affect the speed of evaporation.
- Condensation is the change of matter from a gas to a liquid.

Lesson Review

1. What is water vapor?
★2. Suppose equal amounts of water are outdoors in two open containers. One is tipped over and spilled onto the sidewalk. The other is not. Which water will evaporate faster? Why?

Would You Believe?

Clouds float lower at night than during the day.

152

When does water evaporate fastest?

What you need

water
3 paper towels
small paper cup
watch
pencil and paper

What to do

1. Make a mark 1 cm from the bottom of the paper cup. Add water to that mark. Then, pour the water on a paper towel.
2. Repeat step 1 for each of the other paper towels.
3. Now, fold the first towel in half. Fold the second in half. Then, fold it in half again.
4. Do not fold the third paper towel.
5. Put all three towels in a warm, dry place.
6. Record how long it takes for each towel to dry.

What did you learn?

1. Which paper towel dried fastest?
2. Which towel took the longest to dry?

Using what you learned

1. How would you hang clothes so they dry quickly?
2. Which will evaporate faster—a cup of water or a spilled cup of water? Why?
3. What could you do to slow down evaporation? When would this be useful?

Clouds and Precipitation

LESSON 2 GOALS
You will learn
- how clouds form.
- the names of types of clouds.
- that precipitation falls from the atmosphere.

Are you a cloud watcher? Sometimes clouds can look like people's faces, imaginary animals, or even the hills and valleys of an undiscovered land. Have you ever wondered why clouds form and change?

In Lesson 1 you learned that water vapor can't be seen. But when water vapor condenses on tiny particles of dust in the air, droplets of water form. If the air is cold, water vapor condenses to tiny pieces of ice instead of droplets of water. These water droplets, pieces of ice, or both together make **clouds.**

Cirrus (SIHR us) clouds are thin and white with fuzzy edges. They look like feathers. Cirrus clouds are made of ice crystals. They form high above the ground. You can often see cirrus clouds during nice weather.

What are cirrus clouds made of?

Cirrus clouds

154

Cumulus (KYEW myuh lus) clouds are large and puffy. They are much thicker and lower than cirrus clouds. Cumulus clouds may change shape on a windy day. During nice weather you'll often see scattered, puffy, white cumulus clouds. Low, dark, gray cumulus clouds can bring rain.

Clouds that cover the whole sky are **stratus** clouds. Low, thick stratus clouds may bring rain or snow. A stratus cloud close to the ground is called *fog*.

When can cumulus clouds be seen?

Cumulus clouds

Fog is a stratus cloud.

Precipitation

The water droplets and pieces of ice in clouds are so small that they usually stay in the air. Sometimes the droplets or pieces of ice become large very quickly and fall to the ground. Moisture that falls from the atmosphere is called **precipitation** (prih sihp uh TAY shun).

155

Rain and snow are two kinds of precipitation. When the air is warmer than 0°C, liquid water falls as rain. When the air is 0°C or colder, the water vapor forms ice particles and falls as snow. Sleet and hail are two other kinds of precipitation. Sleet is frozen rain. Hail is ice chunks made of many layers.

If you're a cloud watcher, you may also watch storms. Storm watchers often like to do their watching outdoors where they can see the whole sky. Look at the different sizes of the hailstones in the picture on this page. Why might it be dangerous to be outdoors during a hailstorm?

Lesson Summary

- Water vapor condenses on tiny dust particles to form clouds.
- Cirrus, cumulus, and stratus are three types of clouds.
- Rain, snow, sleet, and hail are four kinds of precipitation.

Hailstones may be different sizes.

Lesson Review

1. How are cirrus clouds different from cumulus clouds?
★2. How are sleet and hail similar? different?

How do amounts of precipitation compare?

What you need
precipitation graphs
pencil and paper

What to do
1. Look at the graphs.
2. Compare the monthly precipitation for Denver and Honolulu.

What did you learn?
1. Which city has the most precipitation during June, July, and August?
2. During what month is Denver driest? Honolulu driest?
3. Which city has the greatest change in amount of precipitation from one month to the next?

Using what you learned
1. What season is Honolulu's "wet season"?
2. What other information is important when comparing climates?

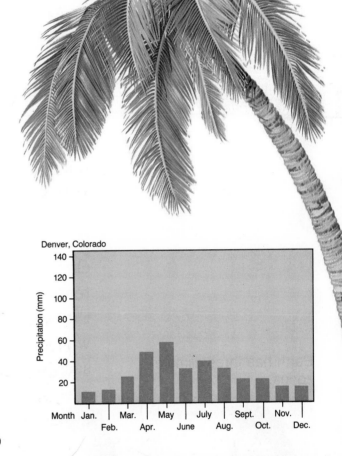

Denver, Colorado

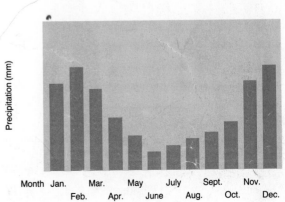

157

Climate

LESSON 3 GOALS

You will learn
- that there are three climate zones.
- that climate is affected by three factors.

What are the three major climate zones?

Did you need a heavy, warm coat last winter? If you did and if you haven't moved, then you're likely to need your heavy, warm coat this winter, too.

From one year to the next, the weather in one place stays pretty much the same. The usual weather in a place year after year is its **climate** (KLI mut).

There are three kinds of climate, or climate zones, on Earth. Look at the picture of Earth on this page. In the far northern and far southern parts of the world are the polar zones. In the **polar zones,** the temperatures are always cold. Centered over the middle of Earth is a climate zone called the **tropics.** Here the temperatures are always hot. The rest of the world lies in the two **temperate zones,** where the weather changes during the four seasons of the year.

Earth has three climate zones.

Different places have different climates because they have different temperatures and amounts of water. The temperatures and amounts of water are affected by three factors.

One of these factors is large bodies of water. Places near oceans or large lakes often receive a lot of rain or snow. These places do not usually have very hot summers or very cold winters. Instead, they are likely to have mild temperatures all year long. These mild temperatures happen because large bodies of water stay cooler in summer and warmer in winter than nearby land areas. Air moving across the water toward land makes the summers cooler and the winters warmer. Temperatures year round are more even. Places far from oceans or large lakes, on the other hand, change greatly in temperature from season to season.

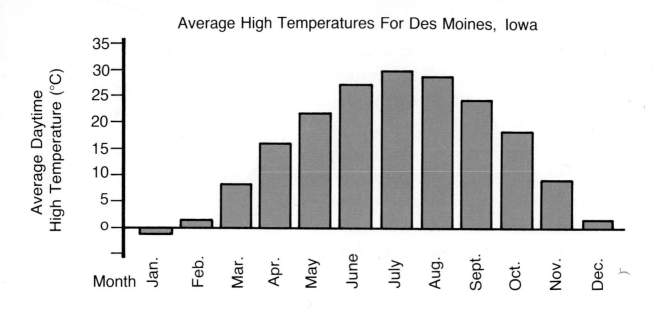

Average High Temperatures For Des Moines, Iowa

Look at the graph on this page. It has temperature information about Des Moines, Iowa. Study the graph carefully. Notice the change in high temperatures during the year. Using this information, would you say that Des Moines is located near a large body of water or not? Why?

The second factor that can affect climate is mountains. They change the wind's pattern. One side of the mountains may get a lot of rain or snow. The other side may have much less precipitation.

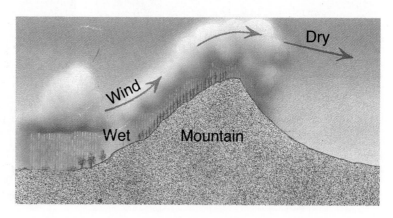

Mountains can affect climate.

The third factor affecting climate is large cities. The number of tall buildings made of concrete and steel in large cities can absorb more energy from the sun than the open areas found in the country. That means that large cities become warmer during the day and stay warm longer at night than open areas of country. Also, the buildings in large cities are often built close together and may cause a change in wind patterns. On windy days the wind may become very strong, making it hard to walk near some buildings. These changes can affect the climate of areas that have several large cities.

How do large cities affect climate?

ACTIVITY

You Can...

Make a Temperature Graph

Contact one of these resources: a local newspaper, the local library, or a local branch of the U.S. Weather Service. Ask for a list of your area's average high temperature for each month of the year. Ask for the average low temperatures as well. Use the information to make two graphs showing these average temperatures.

Now that you know something about climate, where on Earth do you think the climate is the best? Would you enjoy living in a large city? on the side of a mountain? in the middle of an ocean? See what climates your friends like best. Their answers may not match yours!

Lesson Summary

- The polar zones, tropic zone, and temperate zones are three climate zones in the world.
- Water, mountains, and large cities can affect climate.

Lesson Review

1. What is climate?
★2. Would you want to be near a lake on a hot day? Why or why not?

Use with Application Activity on pages 355, 356.

I WANT TO KNOW ABOUT...

A Solar Collector

Polar bears live in the northern polar climate zone. The temperature there is always very cold. Have you ever wondered how polar bears keep warm when it's cold?

Polar bears have fur that keeps them warm. Scientists have found that their fur does a good job of collecting the sun's rays to warm the bear.

Scientists have taken what they learned from studying polar bear fur and used it to make better solar collectors.

A solar collector is a dark material covered by glass. The sun's rays pass through the glass. The dark material absorbs and collects heat from the sun's rays.

Scientists have found that they can collect more heat from the sun's rays if they use fibers that are like the hairs in polar bear fur. When the fibers are put between the glass and the dark material in a solar collector, it allows the dark material to collect more heat.

Science and Technology

Summary

Lesson 1
- Evaporation is the change of matter from a liquid to a gas.
- Air temperature and air speed affect speed of evaporation.
- Condensation is the change of matter from a gas to a liquid.

Lesson 2
- Water vapor condenses on small particles to form clouds.

- Three types of clouds are cirrus, cumulus, and stratus.
- Rain, snow, sleet, and hail are four kinds of precipitation.

Lesson 3
- The three climate zones are the polar zones, tropic zones, and temperate zones.
- Water, mountains, and large cities affect climate.

Science Words

Fill in the blank with the correct word or words from the list.

atmosphere   stratus
water vapor   precipitation
dew   climate
frost   polar zones
clouds   tropics
cirrus   temperate zones
cumulus

1. Ice that forms from water vapor is called ___ .

2. Thick, puffy clouds are called ___ .
3. ___ is water as a gas.
4. Water droplets, pieces of ice, or both form ___ .
5. Clouds that cover all the sky are called ___ .
6. Moisture that falls from the atmosphere is called ___ .
7. Drops of condensed water on grass are called ___ .
8. The air around Earth is the ___ .

Questions

Recalling Ideas

Correctly complete each of the following sentences.

1. The change of matter from a gas to a liquid is
   (a) precipitation.
   (b) condensation.
   (c) evaporation.
   (d) water vapor.

2. Precipitation that is made of layers of ice is
   (a) rain.   (c) sleet.
   (b) snow.   (d) hail.

3. The climate zone centered over the middle of Earth is the
   (a) polar zone.
   (b) temperate zone.
   (c) tropics.
   (d) Antarctic.

4. In the atmosphere, condensation forms on
   (a) sun rays.   (c) rain drops.
   (b) clouds.   (d) dust particles.

Understanding Ideas

Answer the following questions using complete sentences.

1. How do mountains and large bodies of water affect the climate?

2. Compare the different forms of precipitation.

Thinking Critically

Think about what you have learned in this chapter. Answer the following questions using complete sentences.

1. On what kind of day will clothes dry fastest? Why?

2. How do weather changes affect our lives?

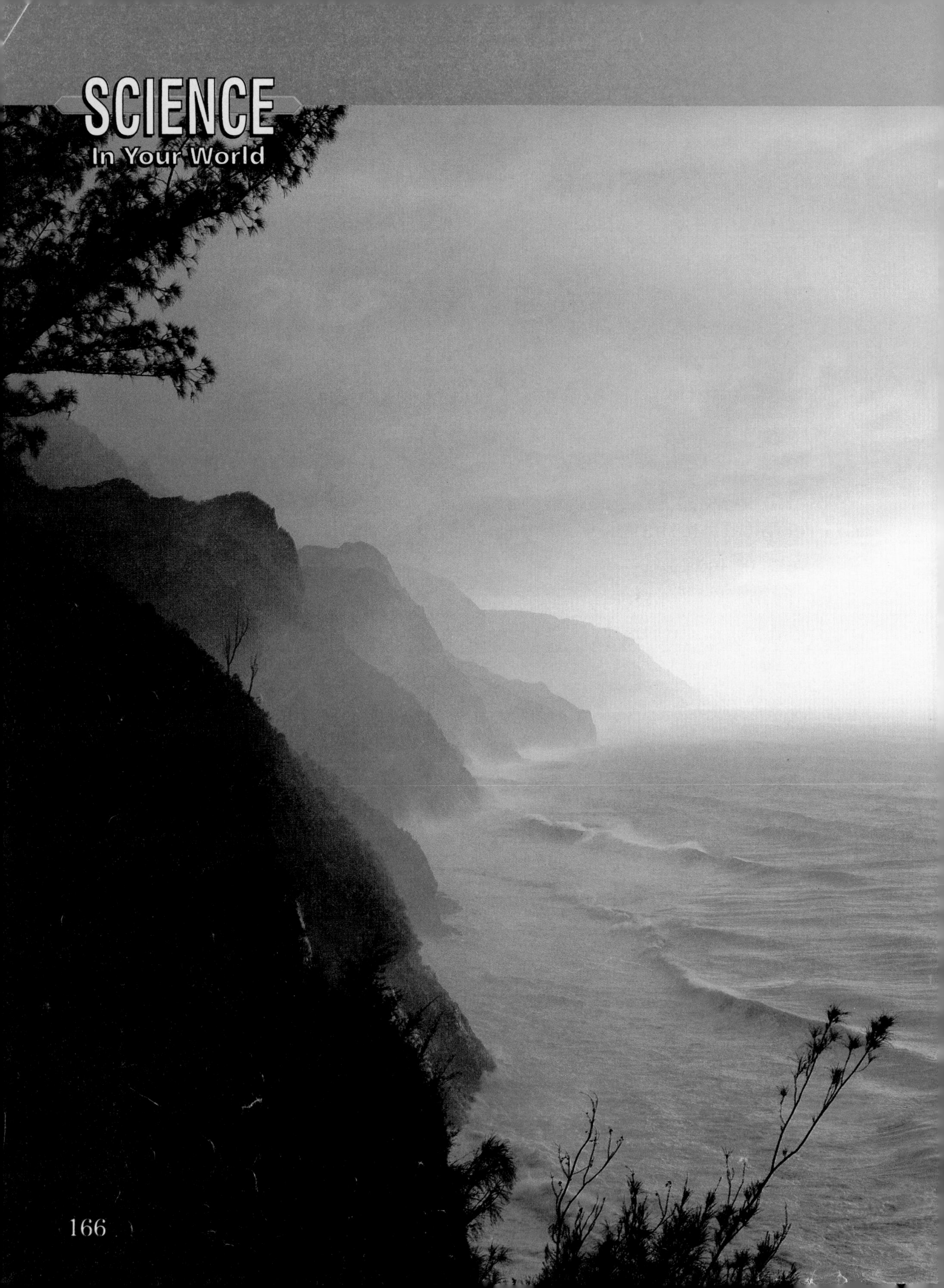
SCIENCE
In Your World

Water

Earth's water is always moving. You have seen it in a variety of places — running out the tap in your bathtub, whistling out of a steamy teakettle, or dripping down the windowpane on a cold morning. Wherever you see water, you see just a small part of the big picture.

Have You Ever...

Followed the Rain?

Have you ever listened to the rain against the windowpane and wondered where it came from? Think about one of the raindrops on your windowpane. Imagine all the places the raindrop has been. How did it get on the window? Where was it before? Has it always been a drop of water? Imagine where it will go when it falls from the window. Write a poem or a story about a raindrop.

The Water Cycle

LESSON 1 GOALS
You will learn
● that water is important to living things.
● the four stages of the water cycle.

Think of all the ways you will use water today. Will you wash your hands? Will you brush your teeth? Will you have a drink of water after recess or before you go to bed? Will you give your plants or your pets a drink, too? Chances are you will use water and not even think about it. Suppose there was no water in your home or school for one day.   How would your life change?

Water is Earth's most important resource. Every living thing on Earth needs water to survive. Without drinking water in some form, you would not be able to live for more than a few days. Think of all the people, plants, and animals near your home. They all need water to survive.

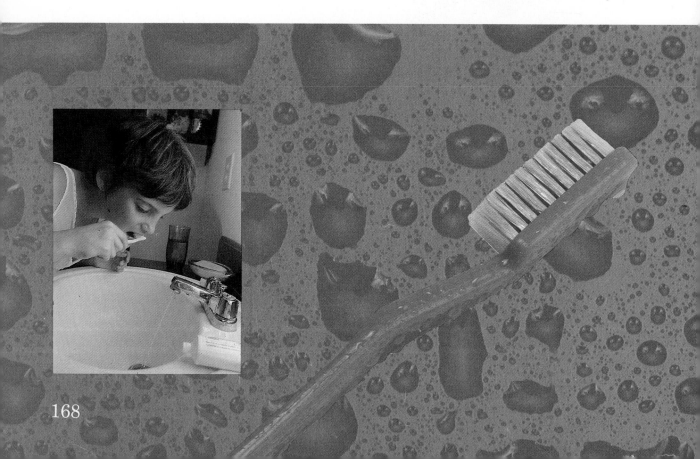

You may be surprised to know that we use the same water over and over. Even though you know that water dries up after a rain, it doesn't just go away. The water just changes form. Water can be solid ice, liquid water, or a gas vapor. In Chapter 8, you learned about evaporation, condensation, and precipitation. Each of these activities is a different part of the **water cycle**. The storage of water on Earth is also part of the water cycle.

What are four stages of the water cycle?

Living things need water.

You Can...

Compare Water Evaporation

Pour a cup of water into two identical flat dishes. Place one dish in the shade. Put the other in direct sunlight. Mark and record the water level in each dish every two hours for a total of six hours. Use the data to write a conclusion. How does direct sunlight affect the speed at which water evaporates?

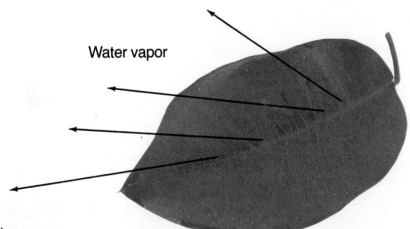

Water vapor

Plants lose water vapor.

You know that a bicycle or a motorcycle moves by spinning its wheels in a circle. The water cycle is the movement of water in a big circle. Water evaporates from oceans, lakes, and streams to form water vapor. Water even evaporates from plants and animals. Heat from the sun provides the energy for this evaporation.

Water vapor then rises into the air. It cools as it rises. Cooling causes it to condense. Condensation changes water vapor to liquid droplets. These droplets join to form rain or freeze to form snow. When the rain or snow falls, water returns to the ground. The water from precipitation flows back into the ground or into streams, lakes, and oceans. Then the cycle is ready to start again. It repeats itself over and over.

Water that gets to our homes was first water that fell to Earth. Then the water may have flowed across the ground or soaked into the ground. Finally it was stored and cleaned for our use.

What changes water vapor to liquid droplets?

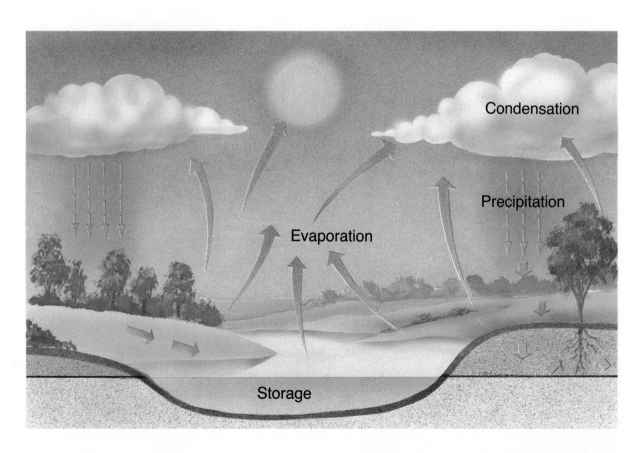

171

Even though rain rarely falls in the Atacama Desert in Chile, plants grow!

Lesson Summary

- All living things must have water to live.
- Evaporation, condensation, precipitation, and storage are stages of the water cycle.
- Earth's supply of water is used over and over in the water cycle.

Lesson Review

1. Why is water our most important resource?
★2. How does the water cycle work?

Energy from sun

What is the water cycle?

What you need

clear plastic glass
oven mitt
hot water
plastic dish
5 ice cubes
pencil and paper

What to do

1. Hold the glass with the oven mitt. Fill the glass two-thirds full of hot water.
2. Tilt the glass to wet the sides to the top.
3. Put some ice in a dish.
4. Set the dish on top of the glass.
5. Observe what happens.

What did you learn?

1. What happened in the glass?
2. Where did evaporation take place?
3. Where did condensation take place?

Using what you learned

1. How does this activity show what happens to some lake water?
2. How does the activity show how clouds form?
3. What process is needed to make this activity a complete water cycle?

173

Runoff and Groundwater

LESSON 2 GOALS
You will learn
• that water moves across and through the ground.
• that gravity causes water to move downward.

Much of the water from rain and melted snow soaks into the ground. Some water flows across the ground instead of soaking in. Water that flows across the ground is called **runoff**. The water running down your street or road after a heavy storm is runoff.

Gravity causes runoff to flow downhill. It flows into small ponds or streams. The streams flow into rivers. Rivers become bigger as more streams flow into them. Finally the rivers flow into oceans. All water on Earth flows toward the ocean.

Where does runoff finally collect?

Runoff

174

Melting snow and precipitation cause runoff. A long, heavy rain can cause a lot of runoff. Melting snow increases runoff. When all this runoff fills streams and rivers, it flows over the banks, flooding the land. Floodwater can carry away soil, trees, and even houses.

Floods cause damage.

Runoff from rain

Groundwater

If you dig a hole in the ground, you will find that deep down the soil is wet. This is because much of the precipitation does not become runoff. **Groundwater** is the water that soaks into the ground.

Gravity causes groundwater to move slowly down into the soil and rock. Water can soak into rock layers deep under the soil. Some groundwater is trapped in spaces in rocks. But most of it moves until it reaches places where it can flow back onto Earth's surface. Lakes, rivers, springs, and swamps are places where water flows back onto Earth's surface. There it may evaporate back into the air or flow toward the ocean.

At what places does groundwater reach the surface?

Lake

Flow of groundwater

Most of us don't think about water very much. We add ice to our drinks. We water the grass. We wash our dishes. And we go swimming without thinking about the water cycle. But if you had a chance to ride the water cycle, you would see things differently. The water cycle would take you on a journey around the world.

Enjoying water

Water flows downward

Lesson Summary

- Runoff is water that flows across the ground.
- Gravity causes runoff to flow downhill.
- Groundwater is water that moves through the ground.

Lesson Review

1. How does gravity affect runoff and groundwater?
★2. How does runoff cause floods?

Which soil soaks up more water?

What you need

2 different kinds of soil
2 large, clear plastic jars
masking tape
marking pen
water
small paper cup
stopwatch
pencil and paper

What to do

1. Fill each jar half full with a soil. Pack down the soil.
2. Label each jar with the type of soil.
3. Pour a cup of water on each soil. Record on your chart how long it takes for the water to soak into the soil.
4. Add cups of water until the soil cannot soak up any more. Record the number of cups.

What did you learn?

1. Which soil soaks up water faster?

Soil type	Soaking time	Number of cups
sandy		
clay-rich		

2. Which soil soaks up more water?

Using what you learned

1. Which soil would have less runoff during a heavy rain? Why?
2. Which kind of soil would have the bigger mud puddles after a heavy rain? Why?

Earth's Water Storage

LESSON 3 GOALS
You will learn
● where water is stored on Earth.
● that careful use of water is important.

"The rain is raining all around,
It falls on field and tree,
It rains on the umbrellas here,
And on the ships at sea."

Robert Louis Stevenson wrote this little poem about the rain. He probably wasn't thinking about whether this rain would be runoff or groundwater. He probably wasn't thinking about how to keep this rainwater for later use. You probably haven't thought much about it either. But these things are very important to life on Earth.

People have different places to keep water until they need it. So does nature. You could keep water in a jar or a thermos with a lid for a long, long time. The hot-water tank in your home or building holds water and keeps it hot for washing.

Rain falls in cities.

Dams hold back water.

Water for people in big cities is often stored in big lakes near the cities. Sometimes people have created these lakes by damming up water from streams or springs. Other times cities are built around lakes or other water sources.

Some ponds, streams, and rivers also store water. Water is often filtered and then pumped through large pipes to tanks in towns and cities. Near your home, you may have noticed a tall tower with a big tank on the top of it. Sometimes the town or city name is written on the tower. These tall tanks are called water towers. Some big buildings have water towers on their roofs. Gravity helps move the water from the tower when it is needed.

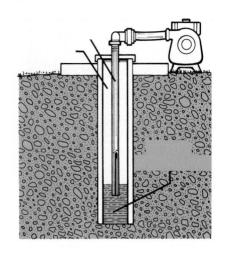

You know that groundwater is often trapped between layers of rock or in holes in rocks. Wells are drilled to get to the stored water. Pumps pull the water to the surface. Many farms and houses in the country get their water from wells.

Water Pollution

Because we use Earth's supply of water over and over, we must store and use it wisely. Each one of the four steps of the water cycle is important: precipitation, evaporation, condensation, and storage. Problems for living things happen when pollution of any of these stages takes place.

Water pollution

For example, water vapor may condense on particles found in some smoke. Then the droplets join and fall to Earth as precipitation. These particles mix with water on Earth through runoff or groundwater. This water can make you and other animals and plants sick or die.

Pollution of lakes, rivers, streams, and other water sources is also a problem for living things. When substances such as oil or sewage get into these sources, the supply of clean water is affected. When any water is polluted, the amount of clean water decreases. The normal supply of clean water cannot be replaced without the pollution first causing harm to living things. The polluted water must be cleaned thoroughly before it can be used again.

Air pollution kills plants.

183

Why is Earth's water so important?

Because there is so much water on Earth, a lot of people think there will always be enough clean water for everyone. Now you know that our water supply is limited. It is important that our water remain clean for our use today and tomorrow. Your help in making sure this happens is important.

Lesson Summary

- Lakes, wells, and water towers are examples of places where water is stored.
- Water in any stage of the cycle must remain unpolluted.

Lesson Review

1. Where do people in large cities often store their water?
2. How does water get polluted?
★3. What would happen if your water supply became polluted?

I WANT TO KNOW ABOUT...

Summarizing the Main Idea

When you write a story, you may use a lot of details to explain what you want to say. But you probably have one main idea in your writing. This is the idea you want your reader to remember. For example, you may tell about a pet you have. But your main idea is that your pet is lovable.

Sometimes writers put the main idea in one sentence. Other times the reader needs to figure out the main idea.

Read the following paragraph. Discuss with your classmates what you think the main idea is.

Drinking water often comes from lakes or rivers. Large pipes carry the water to a water treatment plant. The water is sent through tubes of sand and charcoal to remove the dirt. Chemicals are added to kill germs. The water is then piped to a new, clean storage area. When you need it, clean water is ready.

Language Arts

Summary

Lesson 1
- Living things need water.
- There are four stages of the water cycle.

Lesson 2
- Water runs across the ground and soaks into the ground.

- Gravity moves water downhill.

Lesson 3
- Water is stored in lakes, ponds, streams, and between layers of rock.
- Polluted water hurts living things.

Science Words

Fill in the blank with the correct word or words from the list.

water cycle   **runoff**
groundwater

1. Water that soaks into the ground is ____ .
2. Water that flows across the ground is ____ .
3. Evaporation, condensation, precipitation, and storage are parts of the ____ .

Questions

Recalling Ideas
Correctly complete each of the following sentences.

1. Water first returns to the ground as
   (a) evaporation.
   (b) gravity.
   (c) storage.
   (d) precipitation.
2. Liquid water becomes water vapor through
   (a) precipitation.
   (b) evaporation.
   (c) storage.
   (d) condensation.
3. Water vapor changes to liquid droplets through
   (a) evaporation.
   (b) condensation.
   (c) precipitation.
   (d) storage.
4. Lakes, wells, and water towers are kinds of
   (a) water storage.
   (b) runoff.
   (c) groundwater.
   (d) tanks.
5. Water in wells comes from
   (a) gravity.   (c) groundwater.
   (b) tanks.   (d) rivers.

Understanding Ideas
Answer the following questions using complete sentences.

1. Describe the flow of runoff as it is affected by gravity.
2. Describe the possible movement(s) of water that soaks into the ground as groundwater.
3. How are plants and animals part of the water cycle?
4. How does pollution affect the water cycle?

Thinking Critically
Think about what you have learned in this chapter. Answer the following questions using complete sentences.

1. How is water important to you?
2. Draw a picture to show the water cycle. Label each stage of the water cycle.

187

Checking for Understanding

Write a short answer for each question or statement.

1. How can a glacier change rocks?
2. What type of rock is formed by heat and pressure?
3. Why don't all igneous rocks look the same?
4. In what three ways can water change rocks?
5. Describe the stages of the water cycle.
6. How do water, mountains, and large cities affect climate?
7. What is the difference between runoff and groundwater?
8. How are clouds formed?
9. How is erosion different from weathering?
10. What are two forms of condensation?
11. Where is water stored for future use?
12. What climate zones are found on Earth?

Recalling Activities

Write a short paragraph for each question or statement.

1. How can sediments make layers?
2. How can water break rocks?
3. When does water evaporate faster?
4. Which soil soaks up more water?
5. How does sedimentary rock form?
6. How do different soils compare?
7. How do amounts of precipitation compare?
8. What is the water cycle?

Project Ideas

1. How does pressure affect the formation of sedimentary rocks? Lay books on a few slices of bread. After a week, examine the bread and record your observations. How are the bread slices like sedimentary rock?
2. Make a weather station. Obtain a thermometer and make an anemometer, rain gauge, and weather vane. Record the readings from your instruments.

DINOSAUR

BRONTOSAURUS —
IS A MEMBER OF THE SAUROPODS (THE LARGEST VARIETY OF DINOSAURS). THE BRONTOSAURUS WAS BIG BUT NOT AGGRESSIVE AND SPENT A LOT OF TIME AROUND WATER.
TIME ON EARTH: 150 MILLION YEARS AGO.
JURRASSIC PERIOD.
DIET: PLANTS.
SIZE: UP TO 70 FEET LONG AND 30 TO 40 TONS.

Books to Read

Wonders of Water by Jane Dickinson, Troll Associates: Mahwah, NJ, 1983.
A fascinating question and answer book about water.
Earth by Keith Brandt, Troll Associates: Mahwah, NJ, 1985.
Read this fascinating book about the planet you live on.
Rock Collecting, 2nd Edition by Roma Gans, Crowell Junior Books: New York, 1984.
This book makes rock collecting easy and fun.

SCIENCE FAIR →

Life Science

Feather or fur
Come crawling
Creeping
Some come peeping
Some by night
and some by day.

from "Feather Or Fur"
John Becker

Food for Living Things

As humans, we get our food from many sources—
sometimes from plants and sometimes from meat.

ACTIVITY

Have You Ever...

Played the String Game?

With a ball of yarn, you can see how living
things on Earth provide food for one another.
Write the names of an animal or plant on sticky
name tags and give one name tag to each student.
Now stand in a circle. Choose one person to be
"the sun." That person wraps the yarn around his
or her finger. The "the sun" tosses the ball of
yarn to a plant that makes food because of light. In
turn, that person wraps the yarn around his or her
finger and asks "Who do I provide food for?" Toss
the yarn from a food provider to a food consumer
until everybody has had a turn. What does the circle
look like when the game is over?

Food Producers

LESSON 1 GOALS
You will learn
● that living things need food to live.
● that green plants are food producers.

Think of a time you were really hungry or thirsty. Your body was telling you that you needed food or water. If you don't get these things, you can't live very long. What other things do you need to live?

Just like you, all living things need food and water to live. You also need oxygen to breathe, the right amount of space, and proper temperature. If a living thing's needs are not met, it can't live.

When you think about food, you probably think about foods that taste good. But we don't eat food just because it tastes good. Food is one of the most important needs of living things. Food provides energy for plants and animals. The energy keeps the parts of each living thing working.

Think of all the different foods you eat. Many of these foods are plants or made from plants. You may like peanuts, potato chips, tomatoes, walnuts, rice, green beans, apples, or cherries. Some people even like spinach. All of these foods are from plants.

Green plants make or produce their own food. A **producer** (proh DEW sur) is a living thing that makes its own food. Plants use their green leaves to make food. They need sunlight, water, and carbon dioxide to make this food. Carbon dioxide is a gas that is in air and water. Plants often make more food than they can use. The extra food is stored in the roots, stems, leaves, fruits, and seeds of plants. Think of the plant foods you like to eat. Are they the roots, stems, leaves, fruits, or seeds of plants?

What do green plants use to make food?

The next time you eat, think about the types of plants you are eating. Thanks to these producers, you won't be hungry for long.

Food is stored in many plant parts.

Lesson Summary

- Plants and animals need food for energy to live.
- Green plants can produce their own food.

Lesson Review

1. Why do living things need food?
2. What do you call a plant that makes its own food?
★3. Name foods we eat that come from plant roots, leaves, fruits, and seeds.

What does the plant factory need?

What you need

3 identical bean plants
labels
marking pen
water
metric ruler
pencil and paper

What to do

1. Label the plants **A, B,** and **C.**
2. Add water to **plant A** until the soil is moist. Put **plant A** in a dark place.
3. Add the same amount of water to **plant B.** Put **plant B** in bright sunlight.
4. Do not water **plant C.** Put **plant C** in bright sunlight.
5. Add a little water to **A** and **B** every other day. Measure each plant for 10 days. Record your observations.

What did you learn?

1. Which plant is tall and healthy after ten days?
2. Which plant is tall but doesn't look healthy?
3. Which plant grew the least?

Using what you learned

1. What do plants need to grow?
2. What would happen if you kept the soil soaked with water all of the time?

Consumers

LESSON 2 GOALS
You will learn
- what consumers are.
- the difference between predators and prey.
- the difference between plant eaters and predators.

If you were going to make yourself something to eat, what would you make? Where would you get the food? You might have grown some of it in a garden. Or you might have to go out to buy the food. Either way, your body doesn't make its own food.

Like you, other animals can't make their own food. An animal is a **consumer** (kun SEW mur), a living thing that gets its food from other living things.

Some consumers eat only plants. You may have fed squirrels or some birds with bread crumbs or seeds. Deer, cows, sheep, horses, rabbits, and many other animals eat only plants.

Some animals eat only other animals. An animal that kills and eats other animals is called a **predator** (PRED ut ur). Think of some predators you know about. Weasels, hawks, sharks, and bobcats might be on your list. Their food might include rabbits, mice, birds, fish, and other animals.

What is a predator?

Animals eaten by predators are called **prey.** Plant eaters are often the prey of predators. But predators can also be the prey of other predators. For example, a weasel might be eaten by a bobcat.

Some animals, like people, eat both plants and animals. Think of some of these animals. You may know that raccoons and bears eat fruit as well as meat. You might have seen robins eating insects, worms, and fruits.

Scientists can group some animals as plant eaters or predators by looking at their teeth. The teeth of plant eaters are broad and flat like the back teeth in your mouth. These teeth can mash leaves and grains.

Would You Believe?

The teeth of a white shark are as hard as steel.

199

Predators have pointed teeth like some of your front teeth. These teeth are sharp and can tear meat. Scientists study the teeth of ancient animals such as dinosaurs to tell what kinds of foods they ate.

Producers, consumers, predators, and prey are all important in nature. Almost everything in nature has a natural predator. If birds stopped eating grasshoppers, think of how many more there would be! The grasshoppers would soon eat up all of their plant food. Though birds eat some grasshoppers, they are really helping them survive.

Lesson Summary

- Animals are consumers because they eat other plants or animals.
- Some animals are hunted and eaten by other animals.
- Plant eaters have broad, flat teeth while predators have sharp, pointed teeth.

Lesson Review

1. How is a consumer different from a producer?
2. Explain the difference between predators and prey.
★3. How can scientists tell whether a dinosaur was a plant eater or a predator?

What plant part is eaten?

What you need

glass or wire cage

animal bedding

mixed seeds

lettuce

carrot

water

jar or dish

small, plant-eating animal

pencil and paper

What to do

1. Prepare a cage for the animal.
2. Place plant parts in the cage.
3. Gently put the animal in the cage.
4. Observe and record what, when, and how the animal eats for two or three days.
5. Clean the cage each day and add fresh food and water.

What did you learn?

1. What did the animal eat?
2. When did the animal eat?
3. How did it hold its food?

Using what you learned

1. Suppose your animal got out of its cage. How could information in this activity help you catch the animal?
2. Some animals eat only one kind of plant. If your animal eats many kinds of plants, why is it able to live in more areas than an animal that eats only one kind of plant?

201

Scavengers and Decomposers

LESSON 3 GOALS
You will learn
● that some animals are scavengers.
● that some animals are decomposers.

What do you do with rotten fruits and vegetables? You probably throw these foods away in the trash. A garbage truck may take them to a landfill. They are buried with lots of other trash. Do you know what happens to dead plants and animals in nature?

You know that green plants are producers and that plant eaters and predators are consumers. Two other kinds of living things are also consumers. They help remove dead matter from Earth's surface.

A **scavenger** (SKAV un jur) is a consumer that looks for and feeds on dead plants and animals. Many animals, such as the buzzard, hyena, crab, catfish, and crow, are scavengers. They don't usually kill things. They look for animals that have already died.

What does a scavenger eat?

Scavengers eat dead animals.

A **decomposer** (dee kum POH zur) is a consumer that changes dead plants and animals into simpler matter. You may have seen molds on bread or other spoiled food. These molds change the color and smell of dead plants or animals as decay takes place. Molds are decomposers.

You may have seen a piece of wood that has been broken down so that it crumbles like soil. Farmers and gardeners depend on decomposers to break down leaves, grass, or other mulch into soil. Some bacteria are decomposers. They break down dead matter into very small parts that are returned to the soil.

Decomposers break down dead matter.

203

Many decomposers are too small to see with your eyes. For a long time, the decay of plants and animals was a mystery to people. About four hundred years ago, the microscope (MI kruh skohp) was invented. The word *micro* means "small," and *scope* means "to look." A microscope is an instrument used to make small things look larger. The microscope showed people that there is a world of very small living things. Using a microscope, you can see decomposers at work.

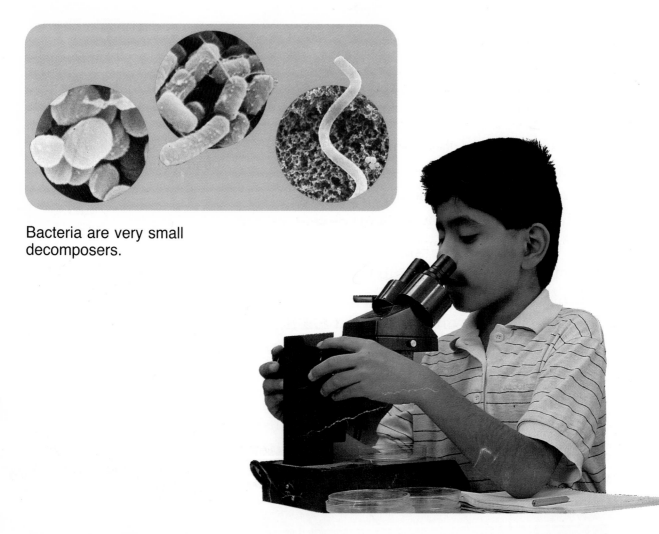

Bacteria are very small decomposers.

You may think scavengers and decomposers do unpleasant work. But their work is very important. They get energy by feeding on dead matter and return that energy to nature. Decomposers put chemicals that were once in living things back into the soil. Without these chemicals, plants could not get the energy to grow and produce food for the rest of us.

Why are decomposers important to plants?

Lesson Summary

• Scavengers eat dead plants and animals.
• Decomposers break down dead plants and animals into simpler matter.

Lesson Review

1. Name two animals that are scavengers.
2. Name two decomposers.
★3. Why are decomposers important?

SCIENCE AND . . .
Math

In 10 spins, what living thing will the spinner probably point to most?

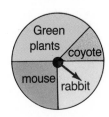

A. Green plants
B. Mouse
C. Rabbit
D. Coyote

Food in a Community

LESSON 4 GOALS
You will learn
● what a food community and food chain are.
● how the sun is important to all living things.
● that energy is transferred from plants to animals.

You live in a community. It may be a suburban community, a farm community, or a city community. A community is a group of people living together in a neighborhood. But you are also part of a nature community.

In nature, a **community** is a group of producers and consumers living together in one area. Every living thing in a community is important. Think of all the living things that might live in a pond community. You might name green plants, insects, fish, frogs, snakes, and bacteria. All of these living things live and work together in the pond community.

Food supplies the energy for living things. But where does this energy come from in the first place? Plants need energy from the sun to grow and live. They use the sun's energy to make food. This energy is then passed on to animals when they eat the plants. The sun is the major source of energy on Earth.

Why is energy from the sun important?

The producers in a pond community are the green plants that use the sun's energy to grow and make food. Some of the energy is passed on to an insect when it eats the plants. The energy that the insect doesn't use is passed on to the frog when it eats the insect. Some energy is then passed on to the snake when it eats the frog.

When the snake dies, bacteria break down the body of the dead snake. The bacteria get some of the energy. Plants then use this energy and more energy from the sun to begin the process again. The insects, fish, frogs, snakes, and bacteria are all consumers in the community.

What is passed on through the food chain?

The energy moves or transfers from one living thing in the community to another. It starts with the sun, then goes to the producers and on to the consumers. All of these living things are connected like a chain necklace. The plant, insect, fish, frog, snake, and bacteria are all links in a **food chain.** Energy, in the form of food, passes through the food chain.

There are many different food chains in each community. Each food chain can have few or many links. A girl eating lettuce from a salad is part of a short food chain. A longer food chain might start with a mouse eating grain. A weasel then eats the mouse. Later, the weasel dies. A vulture eats the dead weasel. When the vulture dies, the decomposers break it down into the soil.

As you take your next bite of food, think about the food chain that you are part of. Is it a long chain or a short chain? What is your role in it?

A person eating a salad is part of a food chain.

208

You Can...

Make a Food Chain

Use 20 cards, yarn, crayons, and a paper punch. Write the name and draw a picture of a plant or animal on each card. Punch a hole in each end of the card. Use the yarn to join the cards together to make food chains. Compare food chains with your classmates. What happens to energy in your chain?

Lesson Summary

- A community is a group of producers and consumers living together in one area.
- The sun is Earth's major source of energy.
- A food chain is the transfer of energy from one living thing to another through food.

Lesson Review

1. What is a community in nature?
2. What is the sun's role in a food chain?
★3. A boy drinks milk from a cow that ate clover. Who are the consumers in this food chain? What is the producer?

Food Webs

LESSON 5 GOALS
You will learn
● what a food web is.
● how energy flows in a food web.

Looking closely at a community, you can see many different food chains. Different animals may eat the same plant. Many predators may hunt the same animal. Consumers eat more than one kind of food. All plants and animals are part of more than one food chain.

What is a food web?

In a spider's web, you can see many fine strings that are all connected. All the food chains put together in a community make a giant web. A **food web** is all the feeding relationships in a community. A food web shows which animals are predators and which are prey. It also includes the scavengers and decomposers.

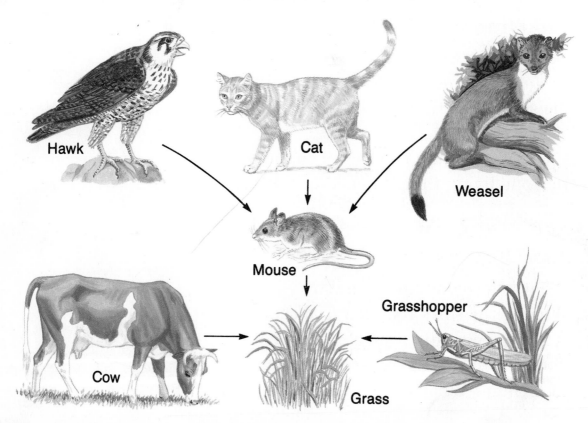

Hawk

Cat

Weasel

Mouse

Grasshopper

Cow

Grass

In each food chain within a food web, green plants produce food. But consumers don't receive all of the energy in this food. The plant uses part of the energy as it grows. The consumer that eats the plant uses part of the energy. Less of the energy from the plant is available to other consumers in the food chain. The energy doesn't go away. It changes its form and isn't available to other consumers.

In a forest community, for example, energy is stored in food made by a green plant. Only some of that energy becomes stored in the body of a deer that eats the green plant. An even smaller part of the plant's energy is then available to a wolf that eats the deer. As energy passes through the food web, living things use a large part of it.

What happens to energy as it passes through the food web?

211

Every living thing in a community is important. They can be members of several different food chains, which make up a food web. Changes in a community cause changes in the food chains and food webs, too. You are a member of your community. The way you live your life makes a big difference to many other living things.

Lesson Summary

- A food web is made up of all the food chains within a community.
- The total amount of available energy from producers is less and less as it flows through a food web.

Lesson Review

1. What is the difference between a food chain and a food web?
★2. How does energy flow in a food web?

I WANT TO KNOW ABOUT...

Artificial Reefs

Do you like seafood? Have you ever had shrimp or tuna? These animals live and find food in the sea. The seafood you see in the grocery store was caught in the ocean and shipped to the store. People who fish are like farmers. They harvest seafood for people to eat. Because seafood is popular, people are looking for new ways to catch more.

Most animals in the ocean live near reefs. Scientists think that if there were more reefs, there would be more seafood to eat. To make an artificial reef, old ships, cars, and even playground equipment have been lowered into the ocean.

Small animals and plants quickly begin to grow on the sunken objects. Soon, crabs and other animals move in, finding food and shelter in the new reefs. Over 400 reefs have been built along the coasts of the United States.

Science and Technology

Summary

Lesson 1
- Living things need food.
- Green plants produce food.

Lesson 2
- Consumers cannot make food.
- Predators eat prey.
- Plant eaters and predators have different types of teeth.

Lesson 3
- Scavengers eat dead things.
- Decomposers break down dead plants and animals.

Lesson 4
- A community is a group of producers and consumers.
- The sun is the major source of energy.
- Energy moves through the food chain.

Lesson 5
- A food web is all the food chains in a community.
- Energy decreases as it passes through the food web.

Science Words

Fill in the blank with the correct word or words from the list.

producer	decomposer
consumer	community
predator	food chain
prey	food web
scavenger	

1. A ___ is all the feeding relationships in a community.
2. Plants and animals live together in a ___.
3. Dead plants and animals are broken down by a ___.
4. A living thing that cannot make its own food is a ___.
5. An animal that eats dead plants and animals is a ___.
6. A ___ kills and eats other animals.
7. Energy in the form of food passes through the ___.
8. A ___ makes its own food.

Questions

Recalling Ideas
Correctly complete each of the following sentences.

1. An example of a decomposer is a
   - (a) root.
   - (b) mold.
   - (c) nutrient.
   - (d) prey.

2. Producers make food with energy from the
   - (a) air.
   - (b) water.
   - (c) soil.
   - (d) sun.

3. All living things need
   - (a) light.
   - (b) food.
   - (c) exercise.
   - (d) carbon dioxide.

Understanding Ideas
Answer the following questions using complete sentences.

1. Tell about the flow of energy through a food web.

2. How do plants make food? Where is it stored?

3. List some animals that are plant eaters, some that are animal eaters, and some that consume both.

Thinking Critically
Think about what you have learned in this chapter. Answer the following questions using complete sentences.

1. Tell about a food web that includes people.

2. A plant—an insect—a frog—a snake is an example of a food chain. Which is the producer and which are consumers?

215

Habitats

Everybody tries to find a home. Ants find a home in the soil. Birds find a home in the trees and cliffs. Fish find a home in the streams and seas. Every living thing needs a place to live.

Have You Ever...

Visited a Pet Shop?

The animals in a pet shop originally came from different places around the world. Go to a pet shop and look at the animals that are there. Find out more about one of the animals by answering these questions:

1. Where did the animal come from originally?
2. What is the climate and weather like there?
3. What are the dangers to the animal in its home?
4. Where would the animal go to find safety?

Using this information, describe the kind of place you would need to provide to give this animal a home.

Habitats Are Important

LESSON 1 GOALS
You will learn
• that each plant or animal lives in a habitat.
• that all living things have special needs.
• that animals can find protection in habitats.

What does a habitat provide?

Could you live underwater in a cave? Could you live in a nest of sticks on the side of a cliff? Of course not! But an octopus lives underwater, and an eagle can live in a nest on a cliff. Could an eagle or an octopus live where you do?

Plants and animals live in all parts of the world. Living things are found in hot as well as cold places. They live in areas that have dry or wet climates. Each living thing lives in a **habitat** (HAB uh tat), a place where its needs are met. A habitat provides the food, temperature, and living space that each plant or animal needs.

There are many kinds of habitats. A robin may have a nest in a tree. A fish may live in part of a sunken ship. A beach pea plant grows near an ocean. The nest and tree are part of the robin's habitat. The ship is part of the fish's habitat. The sandy soil is part of the pea plant's habitat. These habitats are different, but each one meets the needs of different living things.

Each living thing is fit for, or adapted to, its habitat. The water lily and the mole in the pictures on this page are adapted to different habitats. The water lily is adapted to life in the water. How is the mole adapted to life underground?

All living things need air, food, and water. They also need space. If too many plants or animals are in one place, the needs of each living thing cannot be met.

Suppose you planted vegetables in a garden. Not knowing any better, you poured one hundred seeds onto a small area of garden soil. All of the seeds sprouted. At first, all the seedlings grew well. The next week, some of the plants began to turn yellow and wilt. Soon those plants died. The other plants didn't look healthy. The problem was that too many plants were in one small area. No plant had enough water, food, and light.

The same thing would be true if too many foxes were in one habitat. There would not be enough water and food in the space. Not all of the foxes could live there.

Plants need space

Within each living space, animals find shelters. A **shelter** is a place or object that protects an animal. Animals use shelters for protection from wind, rain, and hot or cold weather. They also use shelters to hide from predators. Think about some animals that are prey. What shelters could protect these animals from predators? List as many shelters as you can.

What is a shelter?

Some animals use caves as shelters. Bats, for example, hang from walls inside caves during the daytime. Other animals use holes in trees or rocks, or ledges under the water. Some animals such as insects and spiders hide in the leaves and flowers of plants. Other animals dig burrows or tunnels. Shelters are a part of an animal's habitat.

Bats in a cave

Birds in trees

School of fish

Some animals are protected from predators by living in groups. Herds, flocks, packs, prides, pods, and schools are some names for animal groups. Most predators do not attack animals in a group. They look for prey that is alone. The group, therefore, is like a shelter for each animal.

A group can also protect some animals from storms. Wind and precipitation have less effect on each animal when the animals are huddled together. In this way, too, the group acts like a shelter.

The world has millions of different places to live. For each habitat, there are different plants and animals that are adapted to it.

Lesson Summary

- Each plant or animal is adapted to a habitat, a place where its needs are met.
- Air, food, water, and space are life needs.
- Shelters protect animals from predators and hot, cold, wet, or windy weather.

Lesson Review

1. What is a habitat?
2. Why would sixty seeds planted in a small area probably not grow well?
★3. How are some animals protected by living in a group?

How can you make a land habitat?

What you need

large jar
lid with holes
metric ruler
gravel
potting soil
paper cup
rocks

plants
water
water dish
small animal
animal food
pencil
paper

What to do

1. Add a 3-cm layer of gravel to the jar. Add an 8-cm layer of soil on top of the gravel. Set a few small rocks on the soil.
2. Place the plants in the soil and add water.
3. Add food to the jar.
4. Put the animal in the jar. Replace the lid.
5. Add food and water as needed. Record your observations.

What did you learn?

1. What was the animal's shelter?
2. How do you know if the needs of the plants and animals were met?

Using what you learned

1. How is this habitat the same as or different from the animal's natural habitat?
2. What would happen if you planted these plants in an aquarium filled with water? Why?

Polar, Tundra, Desert, and Grassland Habitats

LESSON 2 GOALS
You will learn
- the names of four different types of habitats.
- that each type of habitat has a variety of plants and animals.

Imagine a cactus trying to live in the Arctic. Its needs would not be met there. Neither could a polar bear meet its needs if it lived in a hot, dry desert. Plants and animals whose needs are alike live together in the same type of habitat.

Polar and Tundra Habitats

Two areas in the far northern and southern parts of the world have very cold climates and are called polar regions. A **polar region** is an area of ice and snow located near the North or South Pole. Very few plants live in the polar regions.

Climate zones

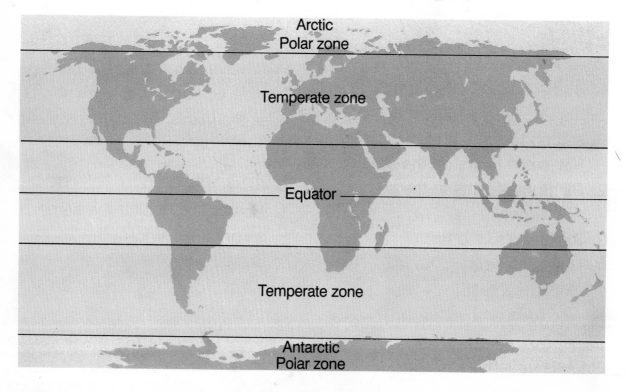

Arctic
Polar zone

Temperate zone

Equator

Temperate zone

Antarctic
Polar zone

Animals of the Arctic tundra

Fish, whales, and seals live in the salt water within both polar regions. Walruses live only in the northern region. Penguins live only in the southern region.

Many kinds of animal life and some plant life are found on frozen land surrounding the ice of the northern polar region. This habitat is called the Arctic tundra (TUN druh). **Tundra** is a cold, dry habitat with a layer of soil that is usually frozen. The tundra is covered with snow more than half the year. The climate is too cold for tall trees to grow. However, small plants such as grasses and mosses do grow in the tundra.

Why aren't trees found in the tundra?

Reindeer

Arctic tern

Musk oxen

The tundra also contains a great variety of animal life. Reindeer, musk oxen, wolves, mice, and the Arctic tern are some animals that live in the tundra.

Some animals living in the tundra grow thick fur in winter and then shed much of the fur in summer. Some animals are adapted to seasonal changes in other ways. Animals such as the Arctic hare have lighter-colored fur in winter than in summer. How does this color change protect the Arctic hare?

226

Desert Habitat

Another type of habitat is the desert. A **desert** is a habitat that has little moisture. Some deserts are hot and dry. Other deserts are cold and dry. Living things there are adapted to life with little water. Some animals, such as rattlesnakes, get all the water they need from their food. Other animals, such as the camel, drink a lot of water at one time. They can live for many days without drinking again.

Desert plants are also adapted to a dry climate. Some plants such as cacti store water in their stems or roots. Many desert plants have small leaves that lose very little water to the air. These plants are able to live for a long time without taking up water.

Camel

Turtle

Cactus

Animals in the desert are adapted to a dry habitat. Living underground is one way animals stay cool in the desert. Small size is an important adaptation to desert life. Small living things find it easier to escape desert heat than do large animals.

Grassland Habitat

Another type of habitat is the grassland. A **grassland** is a habitat where most of the plants are grasses. Some animals that live in grasslands are prairie dogs, pronghorn antelope, foxes, hawks, lions, and kangaroos. Some of the fastest animals on Earth live there. Grasslands are usually large, open spaces. Speed is necessary to escape from predators or to catch prey.

Lesson Summary

- The polar regions, tundra, desert, and grassland are four types of habitats.
- Each type of habitat contains a variety of plants and animals that are adapted to that habitat.

Lesson Review

1. How are the northern polar and Arctic tundra regions different?
2. Describe a plant and an animal that live in a desert habitat.
★3. Give an example of an animal that lives in the grasslands, and tell how it is adapted to life there.

Animals of the grasslands

Forest and Water Habitats

LESSON 3 GOALS
You will learn
● that there are three kinds of forest habitats.
● that there are two kinds of water habitats.

When you think of the word *forest*, what picture comes to mind? Do you see pine trees, maple trees with bright fall colors, or very tall trees? Do you picture moose and owls, deer and cardinals, or monkeys and parrots? All these living things and more can be found in different kinds of forests.

There are three kinds of forest habitats. Each kind of forest contains plants and animals that are adapted to it.

A **coniferous** (kuh NIHF rus) **forest** is a habitat in many northern regions of the world. The growing season is short, and the weather is very cold. These forests have trees with needle-shaped leaves. Most coniferous trees stay green all year. Spruce and fir are two kinds of evergreen trees found in coniferous forests.

Coniferous forest

230

Temperate forest

A variety of animals live in coniferous forests. These animals include mice, beavers, moose, owls, wolves, and woodpeckers.

A **temperate** (TEM prut) **forest** is a habitat that has four seasons—spring, summer, autumn, and winter. Temperate forests contain mostly broadleaf trees that lose their leaves in autumn. New leaf growth does not take place until spring. Oak, maple, and elm trees are examples of broadleaf trees that are common in many temperate forests. Smaller plants such as wildflowers, mosses, and ferns are also found in these forests.

Animals living in temperate forests are adapted to a year with four seasons. Most of the year, they have a good supply of food. In winter, there is less food. Deer, rabbits, mice, and some birds find food under the snow. Other birds must leave their habitats and fly to warmer places where they can find food. Some forest animals such as insects, salamanders, frogs, chipmunks, and bears sleep through most of the winter.

Chipmunk

Praying mantis

Bear

Animals of temperate forests

Salamander

Where are rain forests found?

The third kind of forest habitat is the rain forest. A **rain forest** is a habitat that receives about 250 centimeters of rain a year. Rain forests are found in South America, Malaysia, and Africa and are hot and wet.

Plants grow quickly in rain forests. They are adapted to daily rainfall and even temperatures. Many evergreen plants with broad leaves grow closely together. Most trees grow tall and are covered with vines.

Animals of rain forests

Animals in rain forests are adapted to life among tall plants. Monkeys use their long tails and arms to swing from tree to tree. Large predators have body colors that help them hide when they hunt prey. Look at each animal in the picture on this page. How is each animal adapted to life in a rain forest?

Water Habitats

Much of Earth is covered with water. On Earth there is more water than land. There are two types of water habitats. There are different kinds of plants and animals that are adapted to living in each of them.

Where is fresh water found?

Freshwater habitats are found in ponds, bogs, swamps, lakes, and rivers. Each freshwater habitat has many kinds of plants and animals living there. Some plants and animals live in very cold waters. Others live in warm waters. Some plants and animals are adapted to waters that flow fast. Others are adapted to still water. Water lilies are freshwater plants. Freshwater animals include largemouth bass, beavers, clams, and frogs.

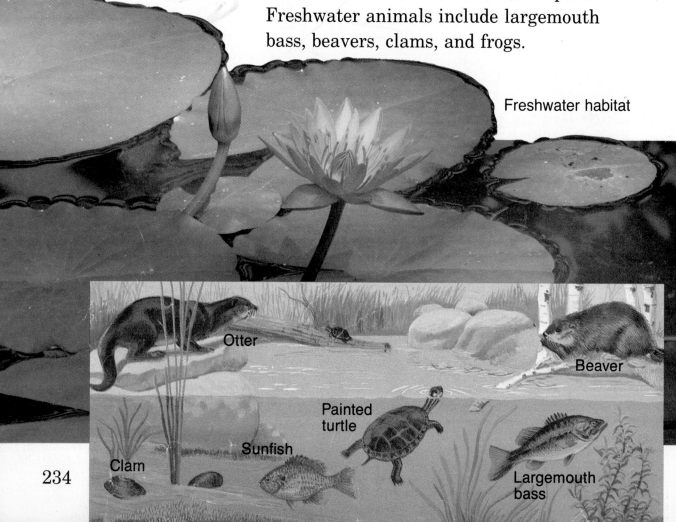

Freshwater habitat

Otter

Beaver

Painted turtle

Sunfish

Clam

Largemouth bass

234

The larger of the two types of water habitats is the ocean or **saltwater habitat.** Large numbers of living things are found in salt water. Some animals such as sharks, jellyfish, sea bass, and whales move freely through the salt water. Sea anemones and sea squirts are attached to objects and do not move away.

Earth has many habitats. Every habitat, even a polar region covered with ice and snow, supports life. All living things are adapted to their own habitats.

Saltwater habitat

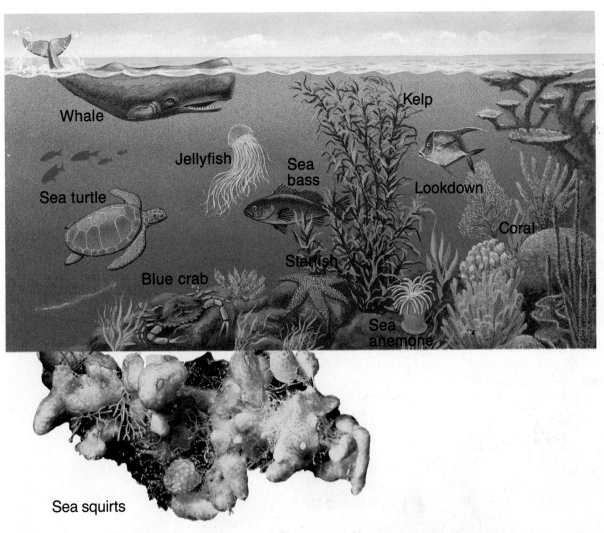

Whale

Kelp

Jellyfish

Sea bass

Lookdown

Sea turtle

Coral

Blue crab

Starfish

Sea anemone

Sea squirts

Lesson Summary

- Northern coniferous forests, temperate forests, and rain forests are three kinds of forest habitats.
- Freshwater and saltwater habitats are the two kinds of water habitats.

Lesson Review

1. Compare the types of trees that grow in northern coniferous forests, temperate forests, and rain forests.
2. Tell about animals that live in temperate forests and coniferous forests.
3. How is a monkey adapted to living in a rain forest?
★4. Describe two animals that live in salt water and two animals that live in fresh water.

What animals live around you?

What you need

rake
mixed bird seed
bread crumbs
peanuts
carrots
flour
metric ruler
resource book on
    animal tracks
pencil and paper

What to do

1. Select a place on the ground where you think an animal lives or visits.
2. Rake leaves away from the area.
3. Measure an area one meter long and one meter wide.
4. Spread flour over the area.
5. Place a variety of foods in the middle of the area.
6. Return the next day and observe any tracks in the flour. Record which foods were eaten.

What did you learn?

1. How many different types of tracks did you find?
2. Where do you think the animal(s) came from?
3. Which food did the animal(s) eat?

Using what you learned

1. What animal(s) made tracks in the flour?
2. How could you use this activity to find out if an animal has made a home in your yard?

People Adapt to Habitats

LESSON 4 GOALS
You will learn
● that people adapt to different habitats.
● that wildlife conservation is important.

You've learned that monkeys live in rain forests, sharks live in salt water, and reindeer live in the tundra. Where do people live?

Most plants and animals live in only one kind of habitat. People, however, live in different kinds of habitats. They adapt to different habitats because they can make changes to them. People can build shelters to protect them from predators and the weather. They can grow and eat different kinds of food. People can make their own clothes. People, like some other animals, can move from one habitat to another. The pictures on this page show different habitats where people live.

Different habitats

ACTIVITY

You Can...

Create a Puppet Show

Use old magazines. Cut out three animals that live in different habitats. You might want to draw your own animals if you can't find pictures you like. Glue each animal to cardboard and attach a cardboard handle. Write a puppet show about each animal. Create scenery for your shows to illustrate each animal's habitat.

Although people make changes to habitats, they must be careful not to harm a habitat. Habitats should remain healthy places for plants and animals. Some people work to protect habitats. Their work is called wildlife conservation. **Wildlife conservation** is the protection that is given to living things and their habitats.

What is wildlife conservation?

Protecting animals

Wildlife conservation should be a concern for everyone. People need to make sure that food chains are not destroyed. Everyone must remember that producers are the basis of every food chain in the world.

Lesson Summary

- People can build shelters, grow food, and travel to different habitats.
- Wildlife conservation concerns the protection of habitats.

Lesson Review

1. What are some examples of changes that people make to habitats?
★2. Why is the conservation of producers especially important?

Use with Application Activity on pages 357, 358.

I WANT TO KNOW ABOUT...

A Zoo Worker

Bill Toone takes care of birds at a large zoo. He is working with California condors, the largest flying bird in the United States. They are seriously endangered.

Condors have lost some of their habitat to humans. Many condors have become sick from eating poison by mistake. The sick adults can't care for their young. People are trying to help.

Some people are carefully taking condor eggs from the nests of sick adults. The eggs are carefully packed and flown by helicopter to the zoo. When a chick hatches, Bill makes sure that it is cared for properly.

Biologists like Bill are working hard to save the California condor. Bill wants to increase the number of condors at the zoo. These birds can later be released to the wild.

Career

Summary

Lesson 1
- Habitats provide the air, food, water, and space that living things need.
- Groups can be shelters.

Lesson 2
- The polar regions, tundra, desert, and grassland are four types of habitats.
- Plants and animals are adapted to each habitat.

Lesson 3
- Three types of forest habitats are coniferous, temperate, and rain forests.
- Freshwater and saltwater habitats are two kinds of water habitats.

Lesson 4
- People change habitats.
- Wildlife conservation concerns the protection of habitats.

Science Words

Fill in the blank with the correct word or words from the list.

habitat✓   coniferous forest
shelter✓   temperate forest✓
polar region   rain forest✓
tundra   freshwater habitats✓
desert   saltwater habitat
grassland   wildlife✓
               conservation✓

1. A forest that has four seasons is called a(n) ___ .

2. A place where a plant or animal lives is a(n) ___ .

3. The protection given to living things is called ___ .

4. A kind of forest with a hot, wet climate is a(n) ___ .

5. A place or object that protects an animal is a(n) ___ .

6. A habitat with soil that is usually frozen is ___ .

7. Habitats found in rivers and ponds are called ___.

8. A habitat with large, open spaces covered with grass is ___.

9. A dry habitat that receives little moisture is a ___.

10. A habitat that is covered by snow and ice all year is a ___.

Questions

Recalling Ideas

Correctly complete each of the following sentences.

1. Animals live in groups to
   (a) attract predators.
   (b) protect themselves.
   (c) build shelters.
   (d) have more space.

2. The tundra is a habitat that does NOT have
   (a) snow.   (c) soil.
   (b) tall trees.   (d) animals.

3. A rain forest is a habitat that is
   (a) cold.   (c) hot and dry.
   (b) dry.   (d) hot and wet.

Understanding Ideas

Answer the following questions using complete sentences.

1. Why do living things need space?

2. How are the two water habitats the same? different?

Thinking Critically

Think about what you have learned in this chapter. Answer the following questions using complete sentences.

1. Describe a plant or animal that lives in each of the land habitats and tell how it is adapted to that habitat.

2. Why should people be concerned about wildlife conservation?

Animal Adaptations

Think about getting dressed this morning. Did you put on a jacket or a sweater? How do you dress if the weather is very hot? How do you dress if the weather is very cold? Wearing different clothes is one way that we adapt to our environment.

Have You Ever...

Wondered About Life at the North Pole?

If you lived at the North Pole, how would you adapt to protect yourself from the extreme cold? What kinds of animals would you expect to find? How would they be different from the animals where you live? Pretend you're a zoologist who has discovered a new animal at the North Pole. Make a diagram of the animal you have found and make some notes about how the animal survives in the cold climate.

Adaptations

LESSON 1 GOALS
You will learn
● how animals survive.
● what animal adaptations are.
● that all animals have skin.

Brrr! Joel shivered, looking out the car window at the wind tossing the treetops. "It looks like a thunderstorm is coming," he thought. "I hope all the wild animals are snug in their beds tonight." Then Joel chuckled. He knew that wild animals don't have beds like his. He began to wonder, "How *do* wild things stay alive in bad weather?" The answer begins with adaptations.

For an animal to live in its environment, it must be able to protect itself and find food. When an animal is adapted to its environment, it is able to live successfully.

Joel decided to go to the library to find out about how animals adapt.

Adaptation

Any body part, body covering, or behavior that helps an animal live in its environment is called an **adaptation** (ad ap TAY shun). Body coverings help protect body organs. Look at the armadillo in the picture on this page. Notice that a hard, protective armor covers its back. The armor is attached in rows so that the armadillo can curl into a ball. This protects its legs and belly if it is disturbed.

What is an adaptation?

247

Skin

Animals need adaptations of body coverings to stay alive. **Skin** is the outer covering of an animal's body. Skin is a body system that protects the organs inside. It also helps some animals keep the correct body temperature. Skin can sense touch and changes in temperature. Skin can hold or release water as needed.

The skin of some animals provides all the protection they need. A frog's skin gives off a liquid that makes its body slimy and hard to hold. Some toads have organs that make poison in their skins. These organs give off a liquid that may harm animals that try to eat them.

Joel smiled. He had learned a little about how wild things stay alive in bad weather. He decided to read more.

Lesson Summary

- An animal must be able to find food and protect itself.
- An adaptation helps an animal live in its environment.
- An animal's skin protects the organs of the body.

Lesson Review

1. What are two ways adaptations help animals survive?
★2. How does skin help an animal survive?

Scales, Feathers, and Fur

Joel decided that wild animals must have adaptations of their skins that help them stay alive. Joel was right.

Many animals have another layer of body covering outside the skin. This layer may be scales, feathers, or hair. Although scales, feathers, and hair look different from each other, they are all part of the skin. The extra layer of body covering gives more protection to an animal.

Scales are small, thin plates that cover the skin of some animals. There are different kinds of scales. In fish, scales can be smooth, rough, or pointed. They are slippery and help fish glide through water.

Snakes have scales that are dry. Most snakes have scales that overlap and stretch apart when the snake moves. Snakes shed their scaly skins as they grow, leaving them in one piece.

What are scales?

Feathers

Feathers are the strong, lightweight outer covering of birds. The close-up picture on this page shows what a feather looks like. Notice how the parts of the feather lock together somewhat like the parts of a zipper. Very little air can pass through a feather.

You may have seen baby chicks covered with soft, fluffy feathers called down. In older birds, down feathers form a layer close to the skin. Down feathers keep a bird's body at the correct temperature, even when it flies through very cold air.

What is the purpose of down feathers?

Many birds must dive or swim in water to find food. The feathers of these birds are covered with a layer of body oil. Oil makes the feathers waterproof. These oily feathers keep a bird's skin dry, keep its body warm, and keep the bird afloat in water.

Fur

All mammals have hair. In some mammals, the hair is a thick covering of soft hairs called **fur.** Fur protects animals from bites and scratches from predators and helps keep them warm. A polar bear is one example. A polar bear lives in a very cold environment where temperatures are often below freezing. The thick fur of a polar bear traps air and helps keep it warm, even when it dives into very cold water.

Some animals are the same color as their environment. This makes them hard to see, because their body colors blend into their surroundings. The snowshoe hare has a brown coat for most of the year. But in winter, the hare grows a white one.

Lesson Summary

• Scales, feathers, and fur are three types of skin coverings.

• An animal's body covering helps keep it warm and provides protection.

Lesson Review

1. Name three types of body coverings that are part of the skin tissue.

★2. How do feathers keep birds warm?

How do fish scales look under a microscope?

What you need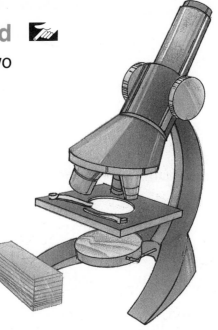

fish scales (from two
    different fish)
microscope
glass slide
coverslip
tweezers
pencil and paper
eyedropper

What to do

1. Prepare 4 slides, one for scales from the upper body and one for scales from the lower body of each fish.
2. Put 2 drops of water on each glass slide. Use the tweezers to put a fish scale in the water. Hold it in place on the slide with a coverslip.
3. Observe each slide under the microscope, first under low power and then under high power.
4. After each viewing, make a drawing of what you saw.

What did you learn?

1. How do the scales look different under the microscope compared to seeing them with the unaided eye?
2. Compare upper and lower scales from the same fish.

Using what you learned

1. Compare the scales of the two different fish you observed.
2. How are scales an adaptation for survival?

Specific Adaptations

LESSON 3 GOALS
You will learn
● about four types of animal adaptations.
● how adaptations help an animal stay alive.

Marlene was carefully trimming the claws of her cat, Woodsmoke. "Are these claws made of the same material as my fingernails?" she wondered. "But they really look different. They're curved, and they come to a point. When her claws get too long, Woodsmoke can scratch her scratching post and remove the whole top layer. It's just like pulling off the top cup in a stack of bathroom cups." Marlene decided she would learn more about cat claws at the library.

What two things must an animal do to survive?

To stay alive in its environment, an animal must protect itself as well as find and catch food. The feet or wings of animals are often adapted for protection and food gathering.

Some body parts that are adapted for protection may also be used for food gathering. For example, an animal might use sharp claws and teeth to protect itself. The animal may also use its claws and teeth for catching food. The eagle in the picture has large wings, sharp talons, and strong foot muscles to catch prey and carry it off.

Some animals, such as the lynx, the arctic fox, and the snowshoe hare, grow extra-long, thick hair on their feet. This increases the size of their feet and helps them move about easily on soft snow to escape their enemies or catch their prey.

The picture of a duck's foot shows how its feet are particularly well adapted for swimming in water in search of food.

Mouth Parts

Some animals, such as sea lions, swallow their food whole. Others have mouth parts for tearing, grinding, or spearing food. The mouth part of a bird is called a bill. Woodpeckers have hard, pointed bills, which they use to chisel or cut into the bark of a tree. Woodpeckers also have long tongues to reach into small openings for insects beneath the bark. Some finches have short, cone-shaped, hard bills. The size, shape, and strength of their bills help finches break open seeds.

Some birds, such as ducks, eat water plants and small insects. These birds have bills with strainers to sift food from the mud and water. Look at the pictures of the different birds. Try to decide from the shapes of the bills which birds are seed eaters, water plant eaters, spearers, or fish-eaters.

Teeth are mouth parts that are used to bite, tear, crush, and grind food. Two long, chisel-shaped teeth at the front of the mouth are found in animals such as mice and squirrels. These teeth are used for biting and gnawing. Cats, wolves, and dogs have long, pointed teeth to stab and tear the meat they eat. Giraffes, horses, and sheep have flat teeth for crushing and grinding plants. What types of teeth do you have?

Marlene was interested by what she had studied about some animal adaptations. "Now, I wonder," she said to Woodsmoke, "if I can find a library book to tell me more about you."

Lesson Summary

- Feet, wings, and mouth parts are three types of animal adaptations.
- Animals must be able to protect themselves and find food in their environment in order to survive.

Lesson Review

1. What are three adaptations that help animals survive?
★2. Explain how a cat's teeth and claws help it survive.

Animal Behavior

LESSON 4 GOALS
You will learn
- about animal behavior.
- about animal behavior that is learned.
- about behavior that animals are born with.

Have you ever tried to train a dog? Dogs can easily be trained to do some things, such as sitting up, begging for food, and chasing thrown sticks. But it isn't so easy to train a dog not to jump up and lick your face or not to eat food left on the coffee table. Why are some things easy and some things hard for dogs to learn?

Everything an animal does is part of its behavior. **Behavior** is a living thing's response to any change in its environment. Anything in the environment, such as light, sound, touch, or smell, can cause a living thing to respond. There are two kinds of behavior. An animal is born with one kind. The other kind is behavior that an animal learns. Both kinds of behavior help an animal survive in its environment.

Learned behavior is behavior that is changed by experience. Learned behavior can be changed. A dog may learn to sit up when its trainer gives a command. Because sitting up is a learned behavior, it can be changed. The sitting-up behavior can be "unlearned." The dog can then learn to do another action when the same command word is spoken. The dog could learn to roll over or put its paw in the trainer's hand in response to the old command. An animal learns a behavior by repeating the same action many times.

What kind of behavior can be changed?

261

On the other hand, animals are born with some behaviors. Ducklings follow their mother. The mother duck leads the ducklings to water. The ducklings can swim without being taught. The picture shows ducklings following their mother to go to swim. Following and swimming are behaviors the ducklings are born with. Behaviors animals are born with can't be changed very easily.

Lesson Summary

- An animal's behavior is everything the animal does.
- Some behavior is learned.
- Animals are born with some behavior.

Lesson Review

1. What are two kinds of behavior a duckling is born with?

★2. What are two kinds of behavior a dog can learn?

Following and swimming are behaviors ducklings are born with.

Reflexes and Instincts

LESSON 5 GOALS
You will learn
● about reflex behavior.
● about instinctive behavior.

What is a reflex?

A baby animal doesn't have to be shown how to drink milk. It already knows. In fact, if you touch a baby animal's nose or mouth, it will try to drink. This is called a reflex action. A reflex (REE fleks) is a simple type of behavior an animal is born with. A **reflex** is the reaction of an animal to something in its environment.

For example, when an animal suddenly sees a very bright light, the animal's eyes blink. This blinking is a reflex action. It's automatic. The animal can't help blinking.

Your eyes have this reflex, too. The reflex happens without your thinking about it. You can see it happen by watching a classmate. You could take pictures of your classmate using a camera with a flash attachment. In all cases, your classmate's eyes will blink.

You have other reflexes, too. For example, you may remember how you jerked your hand away when you touched something hot. This reflex protected you from getting burned. A reflex usually happens very quickly.

Blinking is a reflex action.

Instinct

What is an instinct?

Instinct (IHN stingt) is a complex type of behavior an animal is born with. It is different from a reflex because an instinct includes more than one action. It is also a behavior that can't easily be changed.

Many birds migrate in groups or flocks. The Canada geese flying in a V-shaped formation in the picture are migrating. How do they know where to go? Birds may use landmarks, stars, and the sun to help them find their way. Other animals, such as seals, whales, salmon, and reindeer, also migrate in search of food and a safe place to live and raise their young. How do they know where to go? Instinct tells them.

Spinning a web is an instinct in spiders. They spin webs to capture food to eat. Different kinds of spiders spin different kinds of webs. A spider does not learn to spin a web. Spiders spin perfect webs the first time they try.

Why do spiders spin webs?

Nest building in birds is an instinct. If a bird's nest is destroyed by wind or by another animal during nest building, the bird will build a new nest in the same place. This action may be repeated several times until the young are raised. The bird does *not* learn to build its nest in a new and safer place.

ACTIVITY # You Can...

Build a Nest!

For birds, building nests is an instinctive behavior. You can build a nest, too. Select grass, sticks, leaves, and some mud. Use these materials to create your own bird's nest. Look at examples of real birds' nests. How does yours compare? What kind of bird would most likely make a nest like yours?

Reflexes and instincts are stronger in animals than in humans, but we have them, too. They help us stay alive when there isn't time to think what to do. Animals think much less than humans, but they use reflexes and instincts all the time to tell them what to do next.

Lesson Summary

- Reflex behavior is a simple type of behavior an animal is born with. Reflex behavior is caused by something in the surroundings.
- Instinct is a complex type of behavior an animal is born with. Instinctive behavior includes more than one action.

Lesson Review

1. What are two animal reflex behaviors?
★2. What are two animal instinctive behaviors?

Do mealworms like light or dark places?

What you need
drawing paper
index card
mealworm

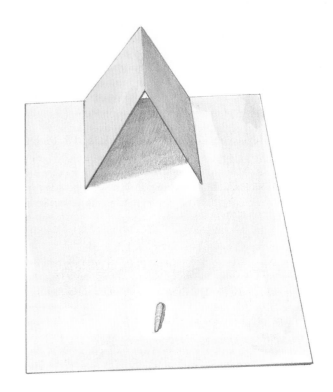

What to do
1. Place the paper on a table. Fold the card to look like a tent and put it at one end of the paper.
2. Put a mealworm at the other end of the paper. Observe and record its movements for 3 minutes.
3. Exchange mealworms with another group of students. Repeat step 2 three more times.

What did you learn?
1. Where did the first mealworm go? the second?
2. How did different mealworms behave?
3. What did other groups discover about how mealworms behave?

Using what you learned
1. What might happen if you had a light shining on the mealworm?
2. How could you set up an activity to find out if mealworms prefer a certain color? Try it and find out.

270

I WANT TO KNOW ABOUT...

Writing the Results

People who study animals spend a lot of time just watching them. They take notes about everything the animals do. Writing these notes acts as a measure of what they see.

Knowing about different kinds of behavior helps in measuring animal actions. All of this information helps people form opinions about how animals behave. The results of their work help people understand why animals behave in certain ways.

Study the picture below and answer the questions that follow.
- What is the brown dog doing?
- Is this a behavior that the dog was born with or has learned?
- What is the cat on the fence doing? Why?
- Is this behavior a reflex or an instinct?

The answers to these questions give general ideas about the actions of different animals. The answers are the results of your study.

Language Arts

Summary

Lesson 1
- An animal must be able to protect itself and find food in order to live in its habitat.
- Anything that helps an animal live in its environment is called an adaptation.

Lesson 2
- Animals have a skin covering of scales, feathers, or hair.
- Skin coverings protect animals and keep them warm.

Lesson 3
- Feet, wings, and mouth parts are three types of adaptations.
- Adaptations help animals stay alive.

Lesson 4
- Behavior is everything an animal does.
- Learned behavior is caused by experience; learned behavior can be changed.

Lesson 5
- An animal is born with reflex behavior, which is caused by something in its surroundings.
- Animals are born with instinctive behavior.

Science Words

Fill in the blank with the correct word or words from the list.

adaptation   behavior
skin   learned behavior
scales   reflex
feathers   instinct
fur

1. A complex type of behavior an animal is born with is called ____ .
2. An animal reacts quickly to something with a ____ .

3. Any body part, body covering, or behavior that helps an animal live in its environment is called a(n) ___.
4. A living thing's response to any change in its environment is ___.
5. Behavior that can be changed is called ___.
6. Small, thin plates covering the skin of some animals are called ___.

Questions

Recalling Ideas
Correctly complete each of the following sentences.

1. An added layer of covering some animals have on their skin is
   (a) bone. (c) wings.
   (b) feet. (d) scales.
2. Learned behavior can be
   (a) skin. (c) an instinct.
   (b) changed. (d) a reflex.

Understanding Ideas
Answer the following questions using complete sentences.

1. What are three extra layers of body covering that come from skin tissue?
2. What is the difference between behavior an animal is born with and learned behavior?
3. Give two examples of a reflex.
4. Give an example of an animal instinct.
5. How does being the same color as its environment help an animal to survive?

Thinking Critically
Think about what you have learned in this chapter. Answer the following questions using complete sentences.

1. How does a cat avoid predators?
2. Describe how one particular animal is adapted for food getting and protection.

Checking for Understanding

Write a short answer for each question or statement.

1. List four needs of all living things.
2. How are producers and consumers different?
3. What kind of animal is a predator? prey? Give an example of each.
4. How are tundra and grassland habitats alike? different?
5. How are saltwater and freshwater habitats alike? different?
6. How can people help to conserve their habitats?
7. What are some things animals must have to live in their environment?
8. What is the difference between behavior an animal is born with and learned behavior?
9. How do decomposers change dead plants and animals?
10. What is the difference between a food chain and a food web?
11. How does fur protect a polar bear in below zero temperature?
12. Name ways in which the following animals are adapted to life in their habitats: camel, bear, antelope, monkey.
13. What happens to energy as it is passed from the producer to the consumer in a food chain?

Recalling Activities

Write a short paragraph for each question or statement.

1. What plant parts are eaten?
2. How can you make a land habitat?
3. How do fish scales look under a microscope?
4. What does the plant factory need?
5. What animals live around you?
6. Do mealworms like light or dark places?

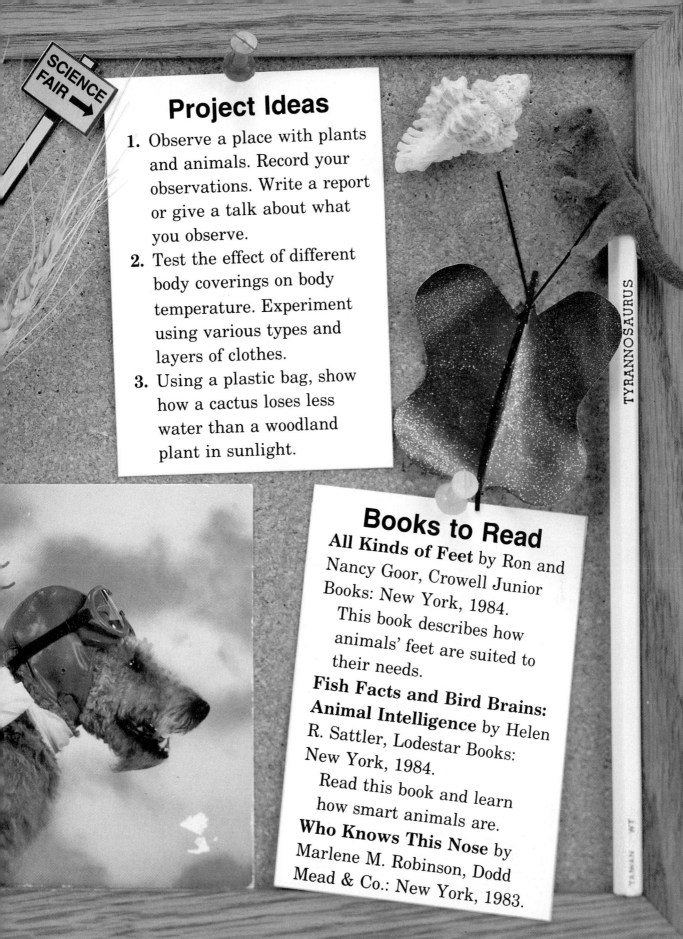

Project Ideas

1. Observe a place with plants and animals. Record your observations. Write a report or give a talk about what you observe.
2. Test the effect of different body coverings on body temperature. Experiment using various types and layers of clothes.
3. Using a plastic bag, show how a cactus loses less water than a woodland plant in sunlight.

Books to Read

All Kinds of Feet by Ron and Nancy Goor, Crowell Junior Books: New York, 1984.
   This book describes how animals' feet are suited to their needs.

Fish Facts and Bird Brains: Animal Intelligence by Helen R. Sattler, Lodestar Books: New York, 1984.
   Read this book and learn how smart animals are.

Who Knows This Nose by Marlene M. Robinson, Dodd Mead & Co.: New York, 1983.

SCIENCE FAIR →

TYRANNOSAURUS

Human Body

Five minutes, five minutes more, please!
　　Let me stay five minutes more!
Can't I just finish the castle
　　I'm building here on the floor?
Can't I just finish the story
　　I'm reading here in my book?
Can't I just finish this bead-chain—
　　It *almost* is finished, look!

from "Bedtime"
Eleanor Farjeon

277

Your Body

Have you ever run in a race with a friend? How did you feel when the race was over? Were your legs tired? Was your heart beating very fast?

Have You Ever...

Tested Your Lung Capacity?

Gather together a dishpan, a jar, a piece of cardboard, and a small length of hose. Pour water into the dishpan until the water is about five centimeters deep. Fill up the jar with water and place the piece of cardboard over its mouth. Put the jar upside down into the dishpan of water. Remove the cardboard and then put the hose up into the jar. Take a deep breath and blow into the hose. What happened to the water in the jar? Why?

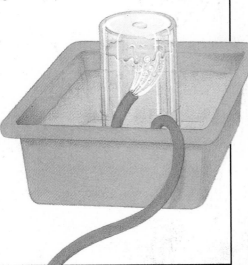

Cells

Have you ever eaten honey fresh from a honeycomb? A honeycomb is the package that bees build out of wax to hold the honey they make. Each boxlike section of a comb is called a cell. The cells are fastened together and are the building blocks of a honeycomb.

Living things are also made of small units called cells. These cells, though, are made of living matter instead of beeswax and honey. A **cell** is the smallest unit of living matter. Most cells are so small that scientists must use microscopes to look at them.

All living things are made of one or more cells. The picture on this page shows an animal cell. All animal cells contain a nucleus, cytoplasm, and a cell membrane. However, all cells do not look the same. They may be round, long, or thin.

Animal cell

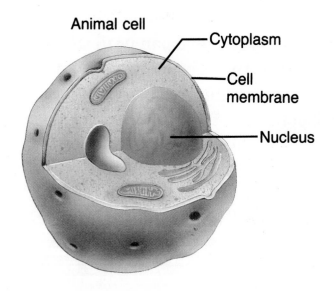

Cytoplasm

Cell membrane

Nucleus

Skin cells

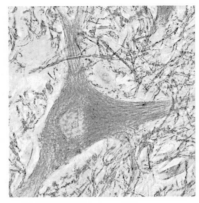
Nerve cells

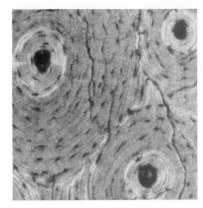
Bone cells

Muscle cells

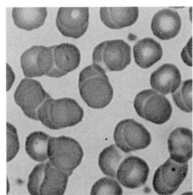
Blood cells

Your body is made of many kinds of cells. Each kind of cell has a different job. A bone cell can't do the job of a skin cell, for example. The pictures on this page show some of the different kinds of cells in your body.

Each person goes through a life cycle that includes birth, growth, aging, and death. Body cells also go through a life cycle. Your body grows larger by adding new cells. New cells form when other cells divide. The new cells grow, divide, age, and die. New cells also replace dead or damaged cells.

Unlike honeycomb cells, body cells don't contain delicious honey. But body cells are also building blocks. They are the building blocks of your body.

Lesson Summary

- A cell is the smallest unit of living matter.
- Different kinds of cells have different jobs within your body.
- New cells grow, divide, age, and die.

Lesson Review

1. How are the cells of your body like honeycomb cells?
2. How does your body grow larger?
★3. What is the life cycle of a cell?

Cells are building blocks.

What do different body cells look like?

What you need
micro-viewer
micro-view slides (human body
    cells)
pencil and paper

What to do
1. Place a slide in the micro-viewer.
2. Observe the cells on the slide. Make a drawing of what you see. Label the cell membrane, cytoplasm, and nucleus.
3. Repeat steps 1 and 2. Continue until all the slides have been viewed.

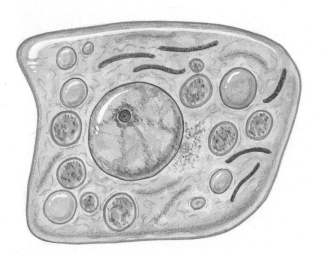

What did you learn?
1. How are all the cells alike?
2. How are the cells different?

Using what you learned
1. Why are there different kinds of body cells?
2. How is a living cell different from a dead cell of the same type?

Tissues, Organs, and Organ Systems

LESSON 2 GOALS

You will learn
- that cells form tissues.
- that tissues form organs.
- that organs form organ systems.

Have you ever watched a school band? All of the members of a band work together as a group so that they all move at the same time. Members of a band are like body cells.

When you raise your hand or breathe in and out, your body cells are working together in groups. Most organisms have more than one kind of cell. Each cell works with others of the same kind. Groups of cells working together are called **tissues** (TIHSH ewz).

Working together

Different kinds of tissues in your body include muscle, bone, skin, nerve, and blood. Muscle tissue tightens and relaxes to perform jobs such as moving a leg or smiling. Other body tissues do different jobs. Nerve tissue carries messages between your brain and other parts of your body. You feel a tap on the shoulder because messages are carried between your skin and your brain.

Organs

Cells form tissues, and tissues form organs. An **organ** is a group of tissues working together. Your heart is an organ. Each kind of tissue has its own job within your heart. One of the tissues in your heart is muscle. Another is nerve tissue. What job do you think muscle tissue has in your heart?

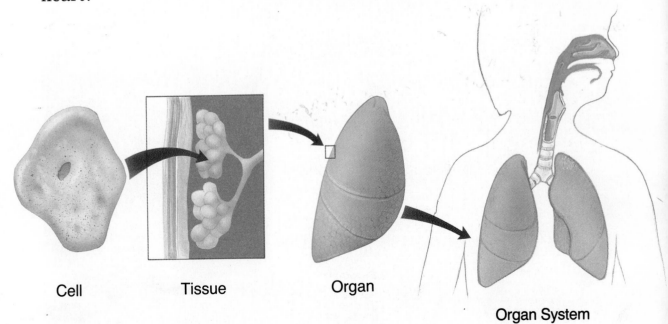

Cell   Tissue   Organ

Organ System

Organ Systems

A group of cells working together forms a tissue. Tissues working together form an organ. A group of organs work together to form an **organ system.** The organs of an organ system carry out a major job in your body. The organs of the respiratory (RES pruh tor ee) system work together to move oxygen from the air you breathe to body cells. Some of the organs of the respiratory system are the windpipe, lungs, and blood vessels. The respiratory system also takes carbon dioxide away from the cells.

What job do all the organs of the respiratory system carry out?

Playing

Working

Your body is made up of many cells, tissues, organs, and organ systems. They all work together so that you can work and play.

Lesson Summary

- Cells working together in a large group form a tissue.
- A group of tissues working together forms an organ.
- A group of organs working together forms an organ system.

Lesson Review

1. What does nerve tissue do?
2. Why is the heart an organ?
★3. Why is the respiratory system important to your body?

Circulatory, Skeletal, and Muscular Systems

The **circulatory** (SUR kyuh luh tor ee) **system** moves blood throughout your body. Your heart pumps blood through blood vessels to all parts of your body with each heartbeat. Blood returns to your heart through other blood vessels. This process is repeated over and over. Blood carries food and oxygen to all parts of your body. It also takes wastes away from body cells.

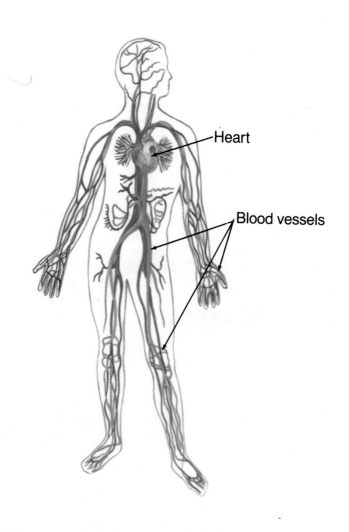

Heart

Blood vessels

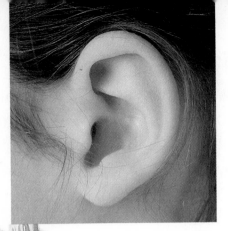

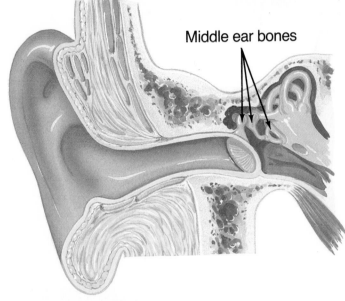

Middle ear bones

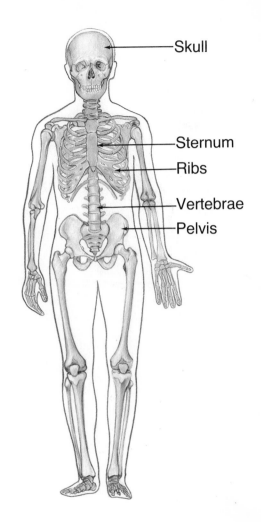

Skull

Sternum

Ribs

Vertebrae

Pelvis

Skeletal System

The **skeletal** (SKEL ut ul) **system** gives your body shape and support. It also protects many organs. The skeletal system is made of bone tissue and other support tissue. Bone tissue forms over 200 bones in your body. Your largest bone is the long bone in your upper leg. The smallest bones are three tiny bones in your middle ear. Bones of your skull protect your brain. Compare the pictures of the body on this page and on page 295. What part of the skeletal system protects the lungs?

Muscular System

The **muscular system** is made of muscle tissue. Your body parts move because muscles and bones work together to make them move. You use muscles to walk, talk, and eat. What else can you do because you have muscles?

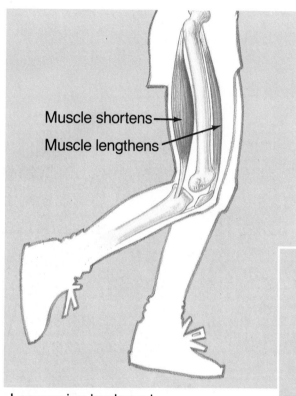

Muscle shortens
Muscle lengthens

Leg moving backward

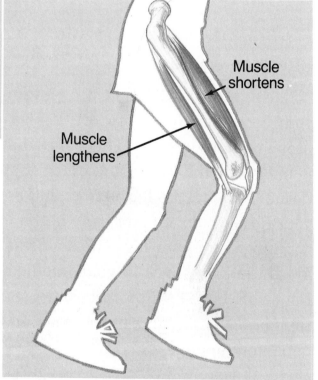

Muscle shortens

Muscle lengthens

Leg moving forward

When a muscle moves a part of your body, the muscle either contracts or relaxes. A muscle shortens when it contracts and lengthens when it relaxes. When you bend your leg, some of your leg muscles contract and other leg muscles relax. When you straighten your leg, the contracting and relaxing of these muscles are reversed. Try bending your leg now. Use your other hand to feel some muscles contract. Feel other muscles relax. Straighten out your leg and feel how the muscles reverse their actions.

Using muscles

Now put both hands on your cheeks. Find some of the muscles that contract or relax when you smile. Now frown, and find muscles that contract or relax.

Lesson Summary

- The circulatory system moves blood to all parts of your body, and it is made up of the heart, blood vessels, and blood.
- The skeletal system gives your body shape and support.
- Muscles move body parts.

Lesson Review

1. What does the circulatory system do?
2. In what three ways is the skeletal system important?
★3. What happens to leg muscles when you bend your leg?

How does your pulse rate change?

What you need

watch with second hand
pencil and paper

What to do

1. Using one hand, gently place your fingers on the side of your neck just below your jaw.
2. Find your pulse.
3. Count your pulse for 10 seconds. Multiply this number by 6 to get your pulse rate for 1 minute.
4. Count your pulse while sitting at your desk.
5. Record this number.
6. Walk quietly around the room for 45 seconds. Repeat steps 3 and 5.
7. Now run in place for 45 seconds. Repeat steps 3 and 5.

What did you learn?

1. When was your pulse the most rapid?
2. When was your pulse the slowest?
3. Compare your results with those of a classmate. How do they compare?

Using what you learned

1. How long does it take for the pulse rate in step 7 to return to that in step 4?
2. Find the pulse at your wrist. Compare this pulse with the pulse at your neck.

293

Digestive and Respiratory Systems

LESSON 4 GOALS
You will learn
- what the digestive system does.
- the importance of the respiratory system.

The **digestive** (di JES tihv) **system** changes the food you eat so that it can be used by your body. When you eat, your teeth mash, tear, and grind food. The small bits of food then move down a tube and into your stomach. As stomach muscles contract, they mix the food with stomach juices. The stomach juices break down, or digest, some of the food.

The mixture of food and stomach juices passes from your stomach to your small intestine, where the digestion of food is completed. Vitamins, digested food, and water pass into your blood through the walls of your small intestine. The leftover food material that isn't digested moves into your large intestine. This solid waste material passes through your large intestine and is finally moved out of your body by muscles.

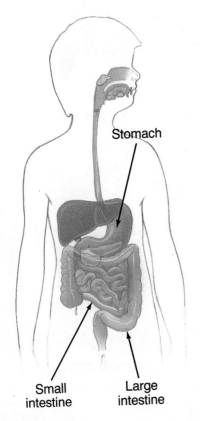

Stomach

Small intestine

Large intestine

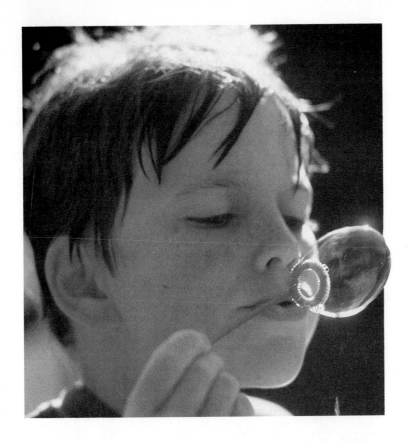

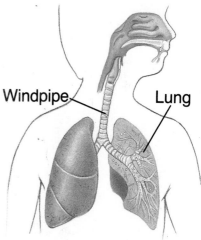

Windpipe | Lung

Respiratory system

Respiratory System

Oxygen and carbon dioxide are important gases. You breathe in oxygen, and you breathe out carbon dioxide. The **respiratory system** makes this exchange of gases happen. All body cells use oxygen to change food into energy. When the energy is formed in the cells, carbon dioxide is made. Carbon dioxide is a waste product. This waste gas is removed from your body when you breathe out.

Why is oxygen important to cells in your body?

You Can...

See Your Lung Capacity

Pull on the sides of a balloon and blow into it several times until it stretches easily. Completely empty the balloon. Now take a deep breath, and blow all your breath into the balloon. Tie the balloon. Look at the size of the balloon. The size shows your lung capacity.

When you breathe in, air enters your body through your nose and mouth. It travels through your windpipe to your lungs. In your lungs, oxygen from the air passes to your blood. Blood carries the oxygen through blood vessels to your body cells. Then the blood carries carbon dioxide away from these cells and back to your lungs. When you breathe out, carbon dioxide leaves your body through your nose and mouth. What is one difference between the air you breathe in and the air you breathe out?

Lesson Summary

- The digestive system changes food so that it can be used by your body.
- The respiratory system brings oxygen into your body and removes carbon dioxide.

Lesson Review

1. Trace food through the digestive system.
★2. How is carbon dioxide formed in the body?

Measuring lung capacity

Urinary and Control Systems

LESSON 5 GOALS
You will learn
● how liquid body wastes are removed.
● that the body has two control systems.

Your body is always producing waste products that are solids, liquids, and gases. Body systems remove waste products so that you stay healthy. The digestive system moves solid wastes out of the body. The respiratory system removes waste gases from your body.

Body cells also produce liquid wastes. Liquid wastes are picked up by your blood. Some of the liquid wastes are released through sweat glands to the surface of your skin. This liquid waste is called **perspiration** (pur spuh RAY shun).

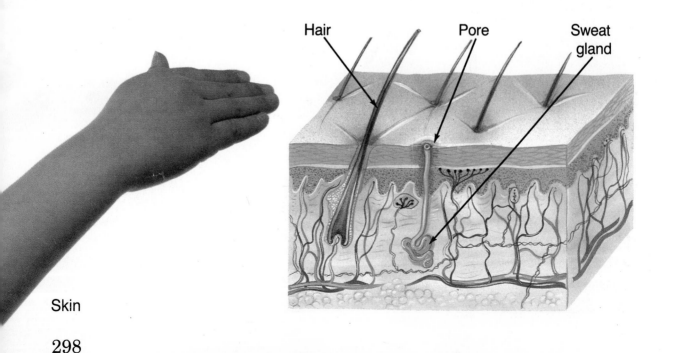

Hair   Pore   Sweat gland

Skin

298

Urinary System

Most liquid wastes are removed from your body by the **urinary** (YOOR uh ner ee) **system.** As blood moves through organs called kidneys, wastes and water are removed from the blood. The wastes and water form **urine** (YOOR un). Urine passes from your kidneys through tubes to your bladder. The **urethra** (yoo REE thruh) releases urine from your body.

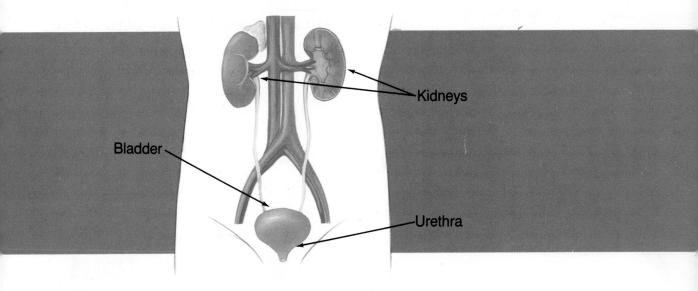

Kidneys

Bladder

Urethra

Control Systems

The control systems of your body keep your body working as one unit. They control your muscles and organs. They control your senses and your thinking. One control system is the **nervous system.** It is made up of the brain, spinal cord, and nerves. The brain and the spinal cord are like message centers.

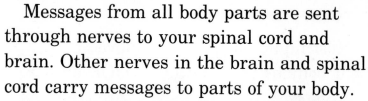

SCIENCE AND . . .
Math

If your heart pumps 395 liters of blood each hour, which is the best estimate of the number of liters it pumps in six hours?

A. Less than 500 L
B. Between 1,500 L and 2,000 L
C. Between 2,100 L and 2,500 L

Messages from all body parts are sent through nerves to your spinal cord and brain. Other nerves in the brain and spinal cord carry messages to parts of your body.

The **endocrine** (EN duh krun) **system** is the other control system. It helps the nervous system control your body and is made up of organs called glands. Glands make chemicals that pass into your blood. Some chemicals are important for proper growth. Others help to digest food.

Each system plays a necessary part. Working together, these systems keep your body growing, working, and healthy.

Lesson Summary

- The urinary system removes liquid body wastes.
- The nervous system and endocrine system are the control systems of the body.

Lesson Review

1. How are solid and liquid wastes removed from the body?
2. How are waste gases removed?
3. What organs make up the endocrine system?
★4. Why are the control systems important to the body?

I WANT TO KNOW ABOUT...

An EMT

Lily Denbo is an Emergency Medical Technician (EMT). She works as part of an ambulance team. When an emergency call is received, Lily and her partner rush to the scene. After giving first aid, they may take the patient to a hospital.

Lily also teaches cardiopulmonary resuscitation (CPR). When a person's heart and lungs stop working, oxygen doesn't reach body cells. Without a normal supply of oxygen, cells will die.

The person trained in CPR works to save a life by helping to bring back the usual action of the patient's heart and lungs. A person trained in CPR can breathe for a patient who is not breathing. The trained person also knows how to get a patient's heart to start beating again. CPR can sometimes keep a person alive until he or she gets to a hospital.

Lily enjoys teaching CPR. She is happy to help people learn to save lives.

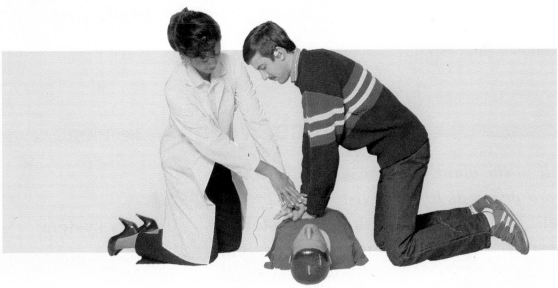

Career

Summary

Lesson 1
- Cells can be found in all living things.
- Different kinds of cells have different jobs.

Lesson 2
- Cells working together in a group form a tissue.
- Tissues working together form an organ.
- Organs working together form an organ system.

Lesson 3
- The circulatory system moves blood through the body.

- The skeletal system gives the body shape and support.
- Muscles move body parts.

Lesson 4
- The digestive system changes food so the body can use it.
- The respiratory system brings oxygen into the body.

Lesson 5
- The urinary system removes liquid body wastes.
- The nervous and endocrine systems are control systems.

Science Words

Fill in the blank with the correct word or words from the list.

cell	skeletal system	urinary system
tissues	muscular system	urine
organ	digestive system	urethra
organ system	respiratory system	nervous system
circulatory system	perspiration	endocrine system

1. A group of tissues working together forms a(n) ____ .
2. The liquid waste released through sweat glands is called ____ .
3. The smallest unit of living matter is a(n) ____ .
4. The control system that is made up of the brain, spinal cord, and nerves is the ____ .
5. Cells working together in groups form ____ .
6. The ____ changes the food you eat so that it can be used by your body.
7. The muscular system is an example of a(n) ____ .

Questions

Recalling Ideas

Correctly complete each of the following sentences.

1. Most liquid wastes are removed from the blood by the
   (a) bladder. (c) urethra.
   (b) kidneys. (d) sweat glands.
2. The skeletal system
   (a) sends messages.
   (b) digests food.
   (c) protects body organs.
   (d) pumps blood to the lungs.
3. Food and oxygen are carried to all the parts of your body in the
   (a) blood.
   (b) bone.
   (c) cells.
   (d) air.

Understanding Ideas

Answer the following questions using complete sentences.

1. What are the control systems of the body?
2. Does a person always keep the same cells?
3. What is the function of the muscular system?

Thinking Critically

Think about what you have learned in this chapter. Answer the following questions using complete sentences.

1. Trace some food through the digestive system.
2. What happens to oxygen and carbon dioxide when you breathe in and out?

CHAPTER 14

Staying Healthy

For your body to accomplish all the work it must do, you must provide it with food that keeps it healthy. Think about the foods that you like to eat. Are they good for you? Healthy foods have ingredients that provide nutrients—the building blocks your body needs to accomplish its work.

ACTIVITY

Have You Ever...

Read a Food Label?

Read the list of ingredients of some of your favorite foods. On a piece of paper, list the ingredients that you think are good for you. How many ingredients did you list? Do you think that this is a healthful food to eat?

Eating Well

LESSON 1 GOALS
You will learn
● why we need good foods.
● which groups of foods are good for us.

What is your favorite food? Do you like pecks of pickled peppers, hot cross buns, or green eggs and ham? You need food to stay alive. But sometimes the foods you like best aren't the best ones for your body.

One way to stay healthy is to eat good foods. Healthful foods provide the energy your body needs to grow and repair cells. Your body uses energy from food to keep tissues, organs, and organ systems working.

The foods you eat affect how you feel every day. People who eat the wrong foods or skip meals may get sick often.

You know that a nutrient is a substance needed by living things for growth. Healthful foods have different nutrients. When you eat, the nutrients are carried to all the cells in your body. Your cells use the nutrients to help you grow and to keep your body healthy.

Unfortunately, not all foods are healthful. Candy, chips, and other foods that contain a lot of sugar or salt are not healthful. These types of foods have few nutrients and don't help your body grow. In fact, these foods can hurt your body. If you eat too much of them, they can damage your teeth or make you overweight.

Eating different foods helps your body get all the nutrients it needs to grow. Think of the different types of food you can eat. Suggestions for servings from the five food groups are listed. These suggestions will give you an idea of the kinds of foods you should be eating to stay healthy. In which groups are your favorite foods? They may be in more than one group.

Table 1   Food Groups and Suggested Servings for Children

Milk	Meat	Fruit-Vegetable	Grain	Combination
1 Serving: 1 cup milk 1 cup yogurt 1 1/2 slice cheese	**1 Serving:** 2 oz lean meat, fish, poultry 2 eggs 4 tsp peanut butter	**1 Serving:** 1/2 cup juice 1/2 cup cooked vegetable 1 cup raw fruit or vegetable	**1 Serving:** 1 slice bread 1 cup dry cereal 1/2 cup cooked cereal	**1 Serving:** 1 cup soup 1 cup pasta dish 1 cup stew, casserole
Servings: 3	**Servings: 2**	**Servings: 4**	**Servings: 4**	**Servings: ***

*These count as servings or partial servings of the groups from which they are made.

You may have heard that "you are what you eat." If you eat good, healthful foods, chances are your body will be good and healthy, too.

Lesson Summary

- Your body uses healthful foods to grow and to repair damaged cells.
- Foods from the healthful food groups have the nutrients your body needs to live and grow.

Lesson Review

1. Why are healthful foods important for the body?
2. What is a nutrient?
★3. Why is a food high in sugar not healthful?

Use Application Activity on pages 361, 362.

What healthful foods have you eaten today?

What you need

food group table
crayons
paper plates
pencil and paper

Meal	Foods eaten	Food groups
Breakfast		
Lunch		

What to do

1. Study Table 1 on page 307. Make a chart like the one shown.
2. List the foods you had for breakfast or lunch in the correct column.
3. Using the crayons and paper plates, make a drawing of the foods you ate.
4. Compare your meal with that of a classmate. Decide whether or not you had a healthful meal.

What did you learn?

1. From which groups did you choose your food?
2. Did you or your classmate have the more healthful meal? How can you tell?

Using what you learned

1. What could you do to make your meal more healthful?
2. Plan a menu of healthful foods for two days.

Being Sick

LESSON 2 GOALS
You will learn
● what disease and immunity are.
● what to do when you are sick.

"When I was sick and lay-a-bed,
I had two pillows at my head,
And all my toys beside me lay
To keep me happy all the day . . ."

Over one hundred years ago, the poet Robert Louis Stevenson wrote these lines about being sick. When was the last time you were really sick? How did you feel? What made you sick? Do you know how you can keep from getting sick again?

Diseases

A **disease** (dihz EEZ) is an illness. Some diseases, like colds, chicken pox, and measles, are caused by germs. Germs are tiny living things that you can't see with your eyes. Other diseases, like heart disease or some cancers, can be caused by smoking or not eating the right kinds of food. No one knows what causes some other diseases.

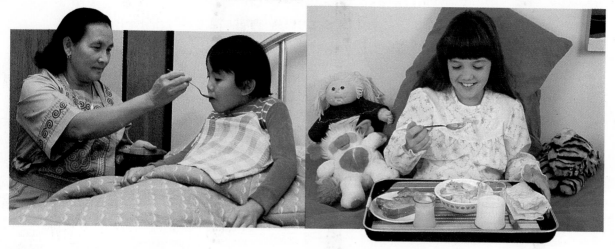

We know that many diseases caused by germs may be spread from person to person. If someone who has a cold sneezes near you, germs may be spread to you through the air. Your hands can pick up a lot of germs just by touching things that sick people have touched. That's why you should wash your hands often. What can you do to keep your cold or flu from spreading to other people?

Your Body's Defense

Even if you come in contact with germs, it doesn't mean you will get sick. Your body has ways to defend itself from germs. Your skin helps keep germs from getting into your body. Tears wash away germs that get into your eyes. Getting enough sleep and eating healthful foods can also help your body defend itself against germs.

When germs do get into your body, they attack your body and harm cells. Your body fights back by making substances that kill the germs. These substances give your body **immunity** (ihm YEW nut ee), or protection, against certain diseases.

What is immunity?

Your body gets immunity in different ways. You can get some diseases only one time. For example, after you have mumps, your body is always protected against the germs that cause mumps.

Sometimes you get a **vaccine** (vak SEEN) to get protection from a disease you haven't had. Vaccines are dead or weak germs that give immunity to a disease. A vaccine can come in the form of a liquid, a pill, or a shot. Babies are given vaccines for diseases like whooping cough, polio, and scarlet fever so that they never get those diseases. Your school probably required that you have certain vaccines before you started school. Unfortunately, we do not have a vaccine for every disease.

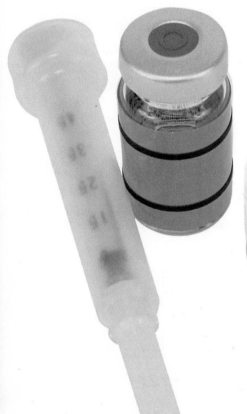

Vaccines come in different forms.

How do you feel when you get sick? Sometimes all you feel like doing is staying in bed and sleeping. When you are sick, it is important to continue to eat healthful foods, stay warm, get rest, and drink liquids.

Healthful foods give your body the energy it needs to repair body cells. Rest and sleep allow your body to heal faster and fight the disease. If an illness continues, you should see a doctor. The doctor may give you medicine to help your body fight the disease. After all, the best thing about being sick is getting well.

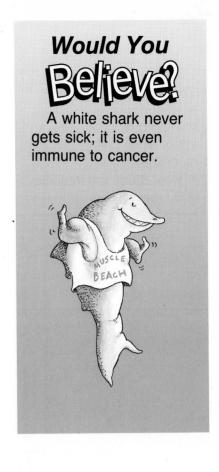

Lesson Summary

- A disease is an illness that can be caused by germs that enter the body. Immunity is the body's protection against certain diseases.
- Liquids, healthful foods, and rest are needed when you are sick.

Lesson Review

1. How do you get diseases like colds or the flu?
2. How can your body become immune to a disease?
3. What should you do if you are ill?
★4. Why should schools make sure that students have certain vaccines?

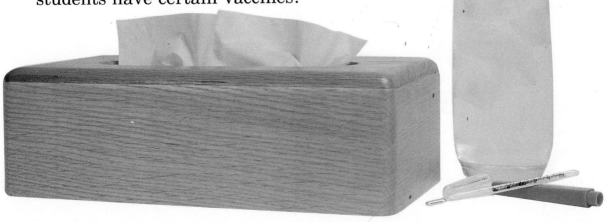

Taking Medicines

LESSON 3 GOALS
You will learn
- what drugs are.
- important safety rules to follow when taking medicines.
- what drugs are in drinks and tobacco.

If you are sick, you may need some medicine to help you get well. You may have been given medicine the last time you had a cold or the flu. Medicines are drugs.

Medicines

A **drug** is a substance that changes the way your body or mind works. Drugs are used in different ways. There are drugs in medicines that cure some diseases. For example, if germs cause an earache, medicines can kill the germs and your ear will stop hurting.

Drugs in medicines can also control, but not cure, some diseases. People with heart disease or high blood pressure may take medicine to control those diseases.

Drugs in medicines can also just make people feel better when they are sick. Cold medicines, for example, will not cure or control cold germs. But they can ease coughing, sneezing, or a runny nose.

314

Medicines are sold in two ways. A doctor must order some medicines. These kinds of medicines should not be taken in the same way by everyone. A **prescription** (prih SKRIHP shun) **drug** is prepared for you after your doctor orders it. An **over-the-counter drug** is one like aspirin and many cough medicines that you can buy without a doctor's order.

Even helpful medicines can be dangerous. It is very important that you follow the safety rules here when taking medicines.

What is a prescription drug?

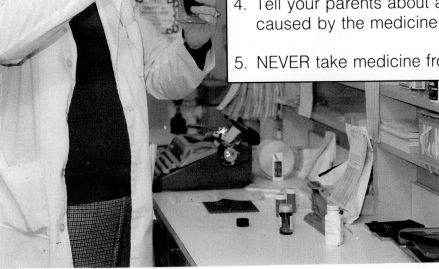

*T*able 2   *Medicine Safety Rules*
1. Take medicine only from your parents, a doctor, or another responsible adult.
2. Do not take anyone else's prescription drug.
3. Follow all directions on the medicine.
4. Tell your parents about any strange effects caused by the medicine.
5. NEVER take medicine from a stranger.

Drugs in Drinks and Tobacco

Not all drugs are medicines. You know that drugs change the way your body or mind works. Some drugs are in common drinks. **Caffeine** (ka FEEN) is a common drug that speeds up the way the body works. Caffeine is in some soft drinks, coffee, tea, and chocolate. Although a lot of people take in caffeine, too much can be harmful to the body. It can keep a person awake at night or make a person feel nervous.

Alcohol (AL kuh hawl) is a drug that slows down the way the body works. Beer, wine, and liquor have alcohol in them. Alcohol can harm body organs and change the way a person thinks or acts. Alcohol may also make people lose control of their muscles.

What effect does alcohol have on the body?

316

Nicotine (NIHK uh teen) is a drug found in tobacco. It is in cigarettes, cigars, and pipe tobacco. It is also found in chewing tobacco. Nicotine speeds up the way the body works and makes the heart beat faster. Nicotine can have the same effects as caffeine.

You can choose not to use harmful drugs. To stay healthy, people choose not to drink caffeine and alcohol. Many people also choose not to smoke or chew tobacco. People who make these choices are working to keep their bodies healthy.

Use Application Activity on pages 363, 364.

317

Lesson Summary

- A drug is a substance that changes the way your mind or body works. Drugs in medicines may be used to cure diseases, control diseases, or to help people feel better when they are sick.
- Five safety rules should be followed when taking any kind of medicine.
- Caffeine and alcohol are harmful drugs found in drinks. Nicotine is a drug found in tobacco.

Lesson Review

1. What safety rules should you follow if you take medicine?
2. What is the difference between an over-the-counter drug and a prescription drug?
★3. How do caffeine, alcohol, and nicotine affect the body?

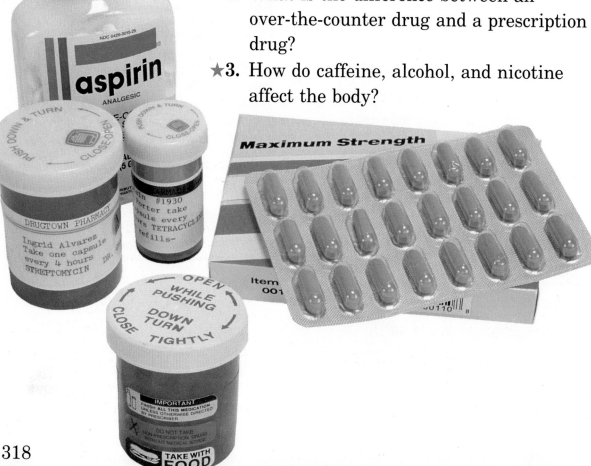

318

How do you know which vaccinations you need?

What you need

resource books and pamphlets
pencil and paper

What to do

1. Look at the list of diseases shown in this chart. Make a copy of the chart.
2. Use resource books. Find out which diseases can be prevented by vaccines. Put an X in column 2 next to each disease that has a vaccine.
3. Find out the age(s) at which the vaccines should be given. Fill in column 3.

What did you learn?

1. Which diseases can be prevented by vaccines?
2. Which vaccines do you need more than one time for complete immunity?

Disease	Vaccine Available	Recommended age
Chicken pox		
Common cold		
Diphtheria		
Heart disease		
HIB (bacterial meningitis)		
Measles		
Mumps		
Polio		
Rubella		
Tetanus		
Whooping cough		

Using what you learned

1. States have laws requiring that all students have certain vaccines before they are allowed to attend school. Why?
2. Show the chart to your parents or guardian. Have you had all of your vaccinations?

319

Poisons

LESSON 4 GOALS
You will learn
- what a poison is.
- important safety rules about poisons.
- what a Poison Control Center does.

"Late at night while you're sleeping
Poison ivy comes a-creeping . . .
You're going to need an ocean of
calamine lotion."

Believe it or not, these lines are part of a song sung by a group called The Coasters. If you have ever had a poison ivy rash, you know what they are singing about. Poison ivy is a pretty green plant that has white berries. If you touch this plant, its oil can cause a painful, itchy skin rash.

Other substances called **poisons** (POY zunz) are harmful if they get on or in your body. Poisons may be solids, liquids, or gases. Like poison ivy, a poison may enter your body through contact with the skin, or you might breathe or eat a poison.

Other plants and some animals are poisonous, too. You can probably think of several insects, spiders, and snakes that inject poisons into a person's body when they bite or sting. Some of these animal poisons can be deadly.

Some gases are poisons and enter our bodies when we breathe them. Gasoline engines produce carbon monoxide, for example. This gas is especially dangerous because it does not have an odor. It could harm you without your knowing it.

Many things that can be poisonous have useful purposes. Often you can find these kinds of poisons in your home. Paint, gasoline, bug spray, and drain cleaner, for example, contain poisons that can be harmful to you. Think of other things that you may have at home that can be poisonous.

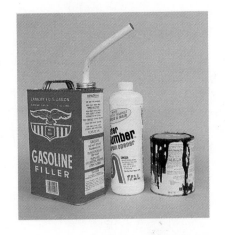

People who make substances containing poisons label the materials clearly, but sometimes the label comes off or is not read. Many terrible accidents have occurred because people have not followed poison safety rules. Since poisons are often found in common places like your home, it is important to follow the five safety rules shown here.

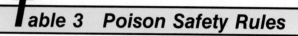

Table 3   Poison Safety Rules

1. NEVER taste an unknown substance.

2. Label all poisons.

3. Store poisons where young children cannot reach them.

4. Read the label before using any product at home.

5. Place the telephone number of your doctor or the local Poison Control Center near your telephone.

What would you do if you or someone you know accidentally took a poison? Many communities have Poison Control Centers that give important information about poisons. They will immediately tell you what to do to get the poison out of your body. The directions given will depend on the kind of poison taken. It is important to place the telephone number of the nearest Poison Control Center near the telephone. Make sure each family member knows where to find this phone number.

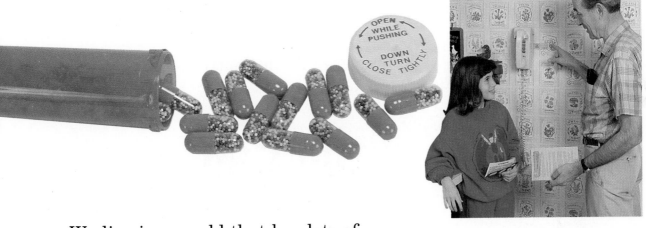

We live in a world that has lots of wonderful things in it. But it has lots of harmful things, too. Will you be the scientist who finds new vaccines or medicines to help people fight disease? Will you be the doctor who helps people learn how to stay healthy? The choices you make about your health today will affect your health in the future. The decisions you make right now can affect your ability to play a helpful role in the world of the future.

Lesson Summary

- A poison is a substance that is harmful. Poisons may be solids, liquids, or gases.
- The five safety rules can help protect you from the harmful effects of poisons.
- Poison Control Centers provide information about what to do if you accidentally take a poison.

Lesson Review

1. Why is it common to find poisons at home?
2. Where can you call to get help or information about poisons?
★3. Why are Poison Control Centers important?

ACTIVITY

You Can...
Design a Poison Warning Sign

Every year many young people become very sick or even die because they tasted something poisonous. You can design a sign that warns people never to taste a poison. Use crayons or paint. Show your sign to the class. How does it warn people about poisons? Where are some good places to display your sign?

I WANT TO KNOW ABOUT...

Dissolving Away Decay

When was the last time you went to a dentist? Did you have a cavity in a tooth? If it wasn't fixed, you would lose your tooth and probably hurt your gums.

You usually don't know if you have a cavity or not. That's why it's important to go to a dentist every six months. A dentist removes the decayed part of the tooth and replaces it with silver or a white plastic material. Teeth that are properly repaired remain healthy for many years.

Having your teeth drilled can be painful. Some dentists use a special liquid that dissolves decay. The dentist squirts the liquid on a cavity, the decay becomes soft, and then the decay washes away. The dentist may still need to use the drill before the tooth is filled.

It is important to keep your teeth healthy so you will have them for a long time. You keep your teeth healthy when you brush and floss every day. Dentists keep your teeth healthy by checking them every six months and repairing them when needed.

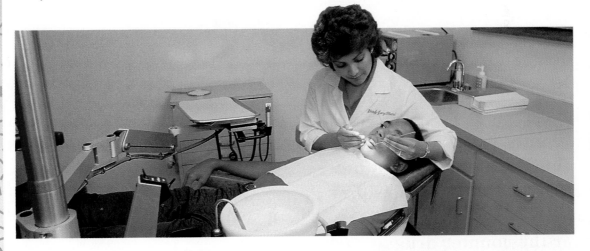

Science and Technology

Summary

Lesson 1
- Healthful foods repair cells.
- Healthful foods have nutrients you need.

Lesson 2
- The body makes substances that kill germs.
- Liquids, healthful foods, and rest are important when sick.

Lesson 3
- Drugs may be used to cure or control diseases.

- Follow safety rules for medicine.
- Caffeine and alcohol are found in some drinks. Nicotine is in tobacco.

Lesson 4
- Poisons are harmful substances.
- Follow five poison safety rules.
- A Poison Control Center can give you information about poisons.

Science Words

Fill in the blank with the correct word or words from the list.

disease	**caffeine**
immunity	**alcohol**
vaccine	**nicotine**
drug	**poisons**
prescription drug	
over-the-counter drug	

1. Harmful substances are ___.

2. An illness is a(n) ___.
3. ___ is found in tobacco.
4. ___ is the body's protection against certain diseases.
5. A drug you can get without a prescription is a(n) ___.
6. Weak germs are found in a(n) ___.
7. A drug in some soft drinks is ___.

8. A substance that changes the way your body or mind works is a(n) ____.

9. A drug a doctor orders is a(n) ____.

10. Beer contains the drug ____.

Questions

Recalling Ideas

Correctly complete each of the following sentences.

1. Carbon monoxide is a
(a) disease. (c) nutrient.
(b) poison. (d) harmless gas.

2. A food from the meat group is
(a) an egg. (c) soup.
(b) milk. (d) cereal.

3. A food from the milk group is
(a) an orange.
(b) bread.
(c) cheese.
(d) peanut butter.

Understanding Ideas

Answer the following questions using complete sentences.

1. How should you take care of yourself when you are sick?
2. List five poison safety rules.
3. List five medicine safety rules.

Thinking Critically

Think about what you have learned in this chapter. Answer the following questions using complete sentences.

1. How do caffeine, alcohol, and nicotine affect the body?
2. Why does the body need healthful foods?

Checking for Understanding

Write a short answer for each question or statement.

1. Why does your body make new cells all the time?
2. What are your body's defenses against disease?
3. What body parts make up the circulatory system?
4. How are medicines helpful to your body?
5. How does your body get immunity?
6. What do muscles do to make body parts move?
7. Give an example of an organ and an organ system.
8. What are five important medicine safety rules?
9. How do caffeine, alcohol, and nicotine affect the body?
10. How might poisons enter our bodies? Give examples.
11. What are five important poison safety rules?
12. What three different things do all animal cells contain?
13. Which organ systems are the body's control systems?
14. What are tissues and what are some examples of tissue?
15. Name the main functions of the skeletal system.
16. What does the digestive system do?
17. What is the main function of the respiratory system?
18. What happens to your body's liquid wastes?
19. What body parts make up the nervous system?

Recalling Activities

Write a short paragraph for each question or statement.

1. What do different body cells look like?
2. How does your pulse rate change?
3. What healthful foods have you eaten today?
4. How do you know which vaccinations you need?

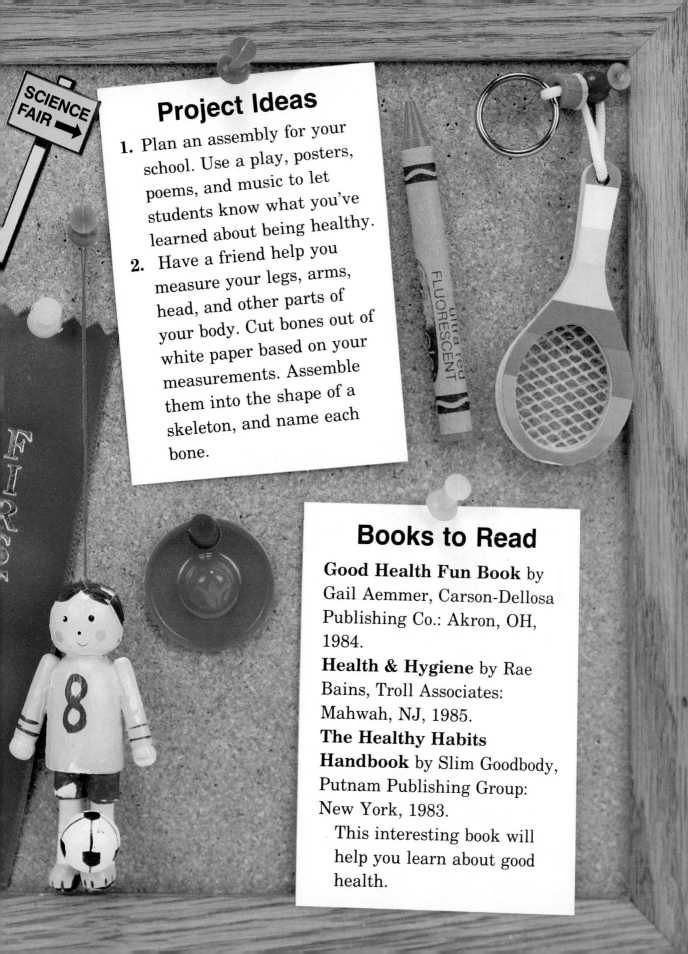

Project Ideas

1. Plan an assembly for your school. Use a play, posters, poems, and music to let students know what you've learned about being healthy.

2. Have a friend help you measure your legs, arms, head, and other parts of your body. Cut bones out of white paper based on your measurements. Assemble them into the shape of a skeleton, and name each bone.

Books to Read

Good Health Fun Book by Gail Aemmer, Carson-Dellosa Publishing Co.: Akron, OH, 1984.

Health & Hygiene by Rae Bains, Troll Associates: Mahwah, NJ, 1985.

The Healthy Habits Handbook by Slim Goodbody, Putnam Publishing Group: New York, 1983.

This interesting book will help you learn about good health.

Activities

Application Activities

Process & Problem Solving Activities

There are many ways to learn about science. You may read or do activities. You use certain thinking skills to observe and record what happens. You use others to explain why something happens. Thinking skills are also used to solve problems. These activities were written to help you practice thinking skills. They were also written so you could use your imagination, to be creative, and to have fun.

TABLE OF CONTENTS

Measuring

Definition   Measuring is finding out the size, volume, mass, weight, or temperature of an object. It is also finding out how long it takes for an event to happen. The object or event is compared to a unit of measure.

Example   Mrs. Boyer used a thermometer to measure temperature. She placed the thermometer on a white sheet of paper. Then she shined a lamp at the thermometer as shown below. The bulb was 15 centimeters from the thermometer. She recorded the temperature each minute. This is what she found.

*M*rs. Boyer's Results

Time	Temperature
At start	24°C
1 minute	28°C
2 minutes	30°C
3 minutes	32°C
4 minutes	34°C
5 minutes	35°C

333

Mrs. Boyer asked the class what would happen if the lamp were shined directly over the thermometer from the same distance. The class decided to find out. Their results are shown below.

Class Results

Time	Temperature
At start	24°C
1 minute	31°C
2 minutes	33°C
3 minutes	35°C
4 minutes	37°C
5 minutes	38°C

Practice

1. How are the measurements taken by the class different from those taken by Mrs. Boyer?
2. What units of measure were used?
3. When might you measure temperature?
4. You can perform this experiment yourself. Make a table like the one below, and record your measurements.

My Results

Time	Temperature
At start	
1 minute	
2 minutes	
3 minutes	
4 minutes	
5 minutes	

Using Numbers

 **Definition**   Using numbers includes ordering, counting, adding, subtracting, multiplying, and dividing numbers.

 **Example**   Mrs. Butler's class had a popcorn contest. Each student started with 50 kernels, which were allowed to pop for three minutes. Timing began when the first kernel popped. Jason found that 45 of his kernels popped. Erica found that 47 of her kernels popped. Here are some more results:

*P*opcorn Popping Contest

Student	Kernels That Popped	Kernels That Did Not Pop
Erica	47	3
Faith	48	2
Jason	45	5
Jodi	46	4
José	40	10
Joseph	46	4
Leroy	39	11
Sarah	38	12

The students looked at the chart. They decided that Faith won. She popped 48 kernels.

335

Practice   Look at the names and numbers in the table on the last page. Answer these questions. Show your work.

1. How many kernels did Leroy and Jodi pop altogether?
2. How many more kernels did Joseph pop than Sarah?
3. Study the information given in the table, then answer this question: How many kernels of popcorn did not pop during the contest?
4. Give examples of how you use numbers at home.

Predicting

 **Definition**   Predicting is proposing possible outcomes of an event or experiment. Predictions are based on earlier observations and inferences.

 **Example**   When Justin took a bath, he put hot and cold water into the tub. He knew that the mixture would be warm. If he put in more hot water, the mixture got warmer. If he put in more cold water, the mixture got cooler.

This led Justin to make this prediction. When equal amounts of hot and cold water are mixed, the temperature of the mixture will be halfway between the temperatures of the hot and cold water. To find out if his prediction was correct, Justin made mixtures of hot and cold water. His results are shown in the table.

Mixing Warm and Cool Water

Temperature of Warm Water	Temperature of Cool Water	Temperature of Mixture
52°C	16°C	35°C
46°C	14°C	29°C
42°C	20°C	31°C
40°C	24°C	33°C
38°C	22°C	30°C

Practice
1. Was Justin's prediction correct? Explain.
2. Suppose you mixed equal amounts of warm water at 36°C and cool water at 20°C. Predict what the temperature of the mixture would be.
3. Test your prediction. How close did you come to your prediction?
4. Do your results support your prediction? Explain.

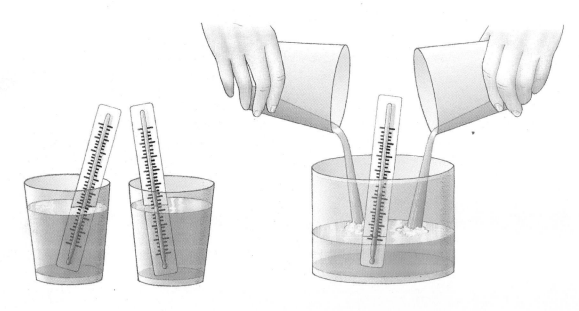

Interpreting Data

 **Definition** Interpreting data is explaining the meaning of information that has been collected.

 **Example** Mr. Hart's students were studying earthworms. They found that earthworms do not have eyes. The students wondered if earthworms react to light.

The students darkened the room. One student shined a flashlight on an earthworm. The earthworm moved out of the circle of light. The same thing happened with each of ten earthworms. The students interpreted this data to mean that earthworms react to light by moving away.

The students then covered the end of the flashlight with different colors of cellophane. Each color was shined on ten earthworms.

*E*arthworm Response
to Light of Different Colors

Color	Response
Red	no worms moved away
Yellow	6 worms moved away immediately; 2 moved away later; 2 did not move away
Green	8 worms moved away immediately; 2 moved away later
Blue	no worms moved away immediately; all 10 later moved away

Practice

1. Look at the table. Which two colors did the earthworms seem to prefer least? Explain.

2. Based on the example and the table, which color did the worms most likely sense as the darkest? Explain your answer.

3. Give examples of the kinds of data you interpret at home or in school.

Controlling Variables

 **Definition**   Controlling variables is making sure that everything in an experiment stays the same except for one factor.

 **Example**   Christopher watched a sugar cube dissolve in water. He wondered if the temperature of the water affected how fast the sugar dissolved.

To find out, Christopher filled two identical cups with the same amount of water. The water in one cup was warm. The water in the second cup was cold. Christopher put identical sugar cubes into each cup. He used identical spoons and began to stir the water in each cup. Christopher stirred each cup exactly the same way. Using a watch, he found out how long it took for the sugar to dissolve in each cup. His results are shown below.

Dissolving a Sugar Cube

Temperature of Water	Time Required
Cold	45 seconds
Warm	20 seconds

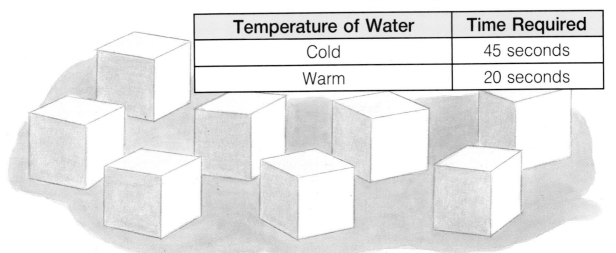

Practice

1. Which variables did Christopher control or keep the same?

2. Which variable did Christopher test or change?

3. What did Christopher discover from his experiment?

4. Design and perform an experiment to see if crushing a sugar cube affects the time required for the sugar to dissolve. Make a table like the one below. What were your results?

Dissolving Sugar

Variables Kept the Same	Variable Changed

Hypothesizing

 **Definition**   Hypothesizing is making an educated guess about how or why something happens. A hypothesis can be tested to see if it is correct.

 **Example**   Jonathan found some small animals called isopods. He found them under leaves in the flower bed. He also found them under rocks near the fence. He did not find any on the sidewalk or patio.

Jonathan formed a hypothesis based on his observations. He suggested that "Isopods like moist places." Jonathan decided to test his hypothesis.

He put ten isopods in the middle of a shoe box. Jonathan sprinkled water on one side of the shoe box to make it moist. The other side was dry. He waited five minutes and then recorded where he found the isopods. Jonathan repeated this experiment four more times.

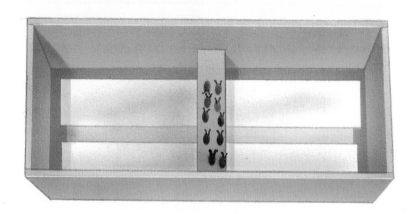

Location of Isopods

Test	Dry Side	Moist Side
1	2	8
2	1	9
3	3	7
4	1	9
5	2	8

Practice

1. What observations did Jonathan make about isopods before he formed his hypothesis?
2. Look at Jonathan's results. Based on these results, was his hypothesis correct? Explain.
3. What other hypotheses can you make about where isopods live?
4. Describe how you would test your hypotheses from question 3.

Who Will Stop the Rust?

Use after page 63.

 Background   Rust is a reddish-brown compound that forms when iron or steel combines with oxygen. Rust is formed when the surface of the iron or steel is exposed to water and air. One way to prevent the formation of rust is to keep these objects dry. Water and oxygen must be kept from combining with the iron or steel.

 Problem   Your class has been discussing the problem of rust. You have begun to list objects that could be damaged by rust, such as cars, bicycles, toys, nails, and tools. The list seems to go on forever! Your teacher has challenged you to devise at least three methods of preventing rust. You are to test each method and decide which is best.

 Materials   objects that will rust, such as washers or paper clips • materials of your choice to stop these objects from rusting • plant mister

Solution

1. Describe the three methods that you will use to prevent rusting.

2. Test your methods by using objects made of iron. Place each object with its rust preventer in a separate paper cup. Place the same type of object in each of three other paper cups. Use a plant mister to spray the objects with water. Do this every day for several days. Record the results each day.

3. How well did your methods of stopping the rust work? Explain.

4. Compare your results with those of your classmates. Which methods worked the best? Why do you think so?

A Balancing Act

Use after page 104.

Background   Every scientist needs basic tools to use for observing and experimenting. One of the basic pieces of equipment is a balance for measuring mass. There are many different types of balances. A simple balance with a pan on each side is one of them.

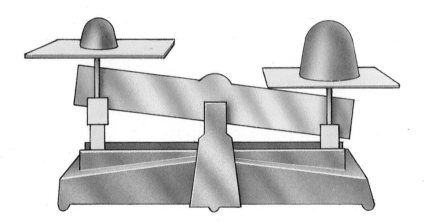

Problem   You are conducting a science experiment. Your experiment involves measuring the mass of some items in grams. Your balance is broken and there is not enough time to go out and buy a new one. You must build a new balance. Your balance must contain at least two of the following simple machines: lever, inclined plane, wedge, pulley, and wheel and axle.

Materials gram masses • blocks of wood • pans or cups for measuring • string • masking tape • flat boards such as rulers • paper clips • drinking straws • clothespins • toothpicks • screws • other materials of your choice

Solution 1. List the materials you will use to make your balance.
2. Describe how you will construct your balance.
3. Draw a picture of your balance. Label the parts.
4. List the simple machines that are contained in your balance.
5. How did you check your balance for accuracy?

An Age-old Problem

Use after page 127.

 Background   Fossils are formed when parts of dead plants or animals become buried in sediments. Over many years, these sediments become sedimentary rock. Sometimes a plant or an animal leaves an imprint in the sedimentary rock. We can study such fossil prints to better understand the features of plants and animals that lived long ago.

 **Problem**   You have found an unusually large leaf. You would like to keep it but know that the leaf will become dry and crumble over a period of time. You decide to use natural materials to make a print of the leaf. You wonder which materials will work best.

Materials aluminum pie pans • water • different types of sediments • interesting large leaves • sawdust • leaf mulch (fine)

Solution 1. Decide which materials you will use. Describe the method you will use.
2. Observe your results. Tell what your print looked like in the natural material.
3. If you used more than one type of natural material and more than one leaf, which material worked best for making leaf prints? Why do you think so?
4. How is the leaf print like a fossil?

Build a Shelter

Use after page 118.

 Background Many rocks and minerals are used for building. Different types of rocks may be used, depending on the environment. Different environments require different types of rocks.

Many modern buildings are made from stones taken from stone quarries. The stones are crushed or cut into smaller pieces. Then they are cemented together over an inner wall of brick or concrete block.

In all cases, buildings made from rocks or minerals must be able to withstand weathering caused by wind, rain, or sand.

 **Problem** Your problem is to build a model shelter. The shelter must be able to withstand wind, rain, sand, and any other elements in the environment.

351

Materials rocks • clay • water • sand • materials of your choice

Solution
1. List the materials you will use to build a shelter.
2. Describe how you will construct your shelter.
3. Build your shelter. Place your shelter outside for one week. After one week, check to see if the shelter has survived the environment. Describe the results.
4. How could your shelter have been improved? Explain why.

Soil Savers!

Use after page 142.

 Background   Soil is important for the growth of crops. Sometimes soil is blown away by wind or washed away by water. Erosion of soil can be prevented in many ways.

 Problem   Your family has just moved into a house that is on a hill. You want to plant a garden, but the rest of your family thinks it will be impossible. They think the soil will erode when it rains. Your job is to build a model of a soil saver to show that erosion near the house can be controlled. You may use natural materials only. No glue or cement is allowed.

 Materials   aluminum pan • soil • water • pan balance • books • paper cups • gram masses • natural materials of your choice

 **Solution** 1. Prepare an aluminum pan of soil as shown:

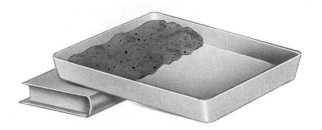

2. Tilt the pan by placing one end of the pan on some books piled on top of each other.
3. Construct a soil saver using natural materials of your choice. Describe your soil saver. Tell what materials you used.
4. Pour 250 mL of water on the soil at the top of your "hill." The soil saver that works the best will be the one with the least amount of soil at the bottom of the pan.
5. Collect the eroded soil at the bottom of the pan. Place the soil in a pan and let it dry overnight.
6. Use a balance to measure the amount of eroded soil in grams. Write the results.
7. Compare the results of your group with those of the rest of the class. Which group had the least amount of erosion?
8. How is the construction of a model important in solving a science problem?

Who Will Stop the Rain?

Use after page 162.

Background
People who live in climates with much rainfall must be prepared for precipitation. They must have plenty of protective clothing. Raincoats, hats, and boots are important to them.

Many different types of materials are used to make weatherproof clothing. Sometimes materials such as plastic or vinyl are used to make this clothing. Also, fabric can be treated with chemicals to make it weatherproof.

Problem
You have gone on an overnight hike with the Outing Club. You have forgotten your raincoat, and a rainstorm is approaching. You need to protect yourself from the rain. All you have is a cotton poncho. There is a supply store nearby that sells things such as candles, plastic wrap, suntan oil, and so on. What can you do to the cloth to make it weatherproof? You may purchase any items of your choice at the supply store.

Materials pieces of cotton cloth • water • pan • spray bottles for water • materials of your choice for weatherproofing

Solution

1. Work in a group. Brainstorm with the other people in your group about materials that could be used to weatherproof a piece of cotton. Record your ideas.
2. Devise three methods of weatherproofing. Describe your methods.
3. Test each method. Spray the protected side of each piece of cotton cloth with water five times. Wait 30 seconds, then turn the cloths over to see which one allowed the least amount of water to go through.
4. Which method worked best? Explain why.

Protect Yourself

Use after page 240.

 Background   Many plants and animals live in only one kind of habitat. People are able to adapt to many different kinds of habitats. One of the things people can do to adapt to certain habitats is to dress differently. It is necessary for people to protect themselves from many different types of conditions within a habitat.

Problem   You have received an award for becoming the Junior Scientist of the Year. You and four other Junior Scientists have been chosen to go with a group of five scientists to study some animals in five different habitats. Each Junior Scientist will go to one of the following habitats: grassland, temperate forest, desert, tundra, and rain forest. You will need to wear the proper clothing and any additional protection necessary to adapt to living out in the open in the habitat you will be studying.

Materials   List the materials of your choice.

Solution 1. Work in a group. Your teacher will assign a habitat to your group. Write the name of your group's habitat.

2. Brainstorm with the members of your group about how you will protect yourself within the environment. Think about things such as temperature, plant and animal life, and resources. Then think of the proper type of clothing to use within the habitat. Choose one member of your group to be the model. Then write a description of the habitat and the type of clothing you will use.

3. Compare the clothing of your group to that of the other groups. How is your clothing the same? How is it different?

4. How will the clothing you have chosen help you adapt to your habitat?

Blending Right In

Use after page 252.

 Background   Some animals blend into their environment so well they can hardly be seen. The ability to hide in this way is called camouflage. Camouflage is an adaptation that helps animals to survive by blending into the environment. Probably the best example of camouflage is the chameleon. This lizard-like creature can change its skin color to blend into different environments.

 **Problem**   Several flying saucers have landed at the edge of your school grounds. Small creatures have come out of the saucers. You are not sure whether or not these creatures are friendly. In order to get a better look at them, you decide to camouflage yourself in the bushes or trees nearest the school building. How can you dress so that you will not be seen by the space creatures?

Materials old clothing of different colors • pieces of cloth that are disposable • scissors • string • materials of your choice

Solution
1. Examine the area near your school building. List the areas in which you can hide.
2. Describe the color clothing you would need to blend in with these surroundings.
3. Create your camouflage clothing. Describe it.
4. Make the table shown below. Then hide in the area you have chosen. Ask several classmates to determine whether or not you are visible at the distances shown in the table. Describe the results of these observations.

*V*isibility of Camouflaged Students

Distances	Results
a. the edge of the school grounds	
b. several hundred meters	
c. less than one hundred meters	
d. less than ten meters	

5. Do you think you could safely observe the space creatures? Explain why. If not, what changes would you make in your camouflage?

What's For Lunch?

Use after page 308.

Background Your body needs nutrients that come from the healthful food groups. Children through the age of 12 should eat the following servings from each of these food groups: milk group: 3 servings, meat group: 2 servings, fruit-vegetable group: 4 servings, and grain group: 4 servings. Each meal that you eat for breakfast, lunch, and dinner should have a combination of servings from these food groups.

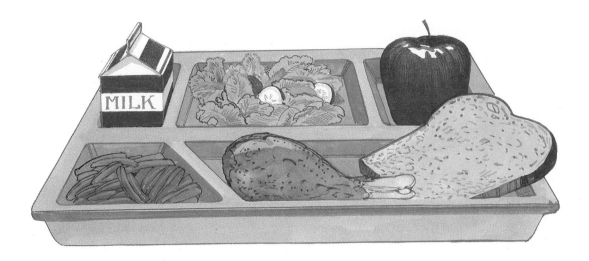

Problem You forgot to bring your lunch to school. You have only $1.50 in your pocket. You want to have a healthful lunch. Look at the cafeteria menu on the next page. Choose a lunch that is healthful and does not cost more than $1.50.

Materials play money

Solution 1. List what you will buy for lunch. Make sure you do not spend more than $1.50.

*D*aily Menu

carton of milk yogurt cheese slice	$0.35 $0.49 $0.10
hard-boiled egg tuna fish sandwich chicken drumstick	$0.25 $0.40 $0.39
carton of juice fruit cup vegetable soup	$0.35 $0.59 $0.49
roll biscuit spaghetti	$0.10 $0.15 $0.45
chocolate cake apple vanilla pudding brownie	$0.25 $0.25 $0.25 $0.25

2. Next to each choice you listed in #1, write the name of the food group to which the item belongs.

3. How can you decide whether or not you had a healthful lunch?

Read the Labels

Use after page 317.

 **Background**   Many people buy over-the-counter medicines when they have coughs or colds. The medicines can help them feel better. They must read the label carefully to find out how much of the medicine to take. They must also find out how often to take the medicine.

 **Problem**   You are helping your mother clean out the medicine cabinet. There are several bottles of cold and cough medicines on the shelf. Your mother asks you to read the labels on the bottles and keep only the bottles of cold and cough medicines that you know can be used for all members of the family, including your 3-year-old sister. You are to throw all the other bottles away. Look at the dosage information from the five medicine labels in the table.

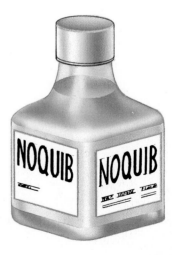

Materials medicine labels

*M*edicines—*Dosage for 24 Hours*

Age	A	B	C	D	E
0-1	Consult Doctor	Don't take	Consult Doctor	Consult Doctor	Consult Doctor
2-3	Consult Doctor	Consult Doctor	5 mL	1 tbs.	Consult Doctor
4-5	Consult Doctor	Consult Doctor	7.5 mL	2 tbs.	Consult Doctor
6-8	2 tablets	1 tsp.	10 mL	2 tbs.	1 tsp.
9-10	2.5 tablets	2 tsp.	12.5 mL	3 tbs.	1 tsp.
11	3 tablets	2 tsp.	15 mL	3 tbs.	1 tsp.
12+	4 tablets	2 tbs.	20 mL	4tbs.	1 tsp.

Solution

1. List the bottles of medicine that you will keep.
2. List the bottles of medicine that you will throw away.
3. What dosage of each medicine could you now take safely?

   Medicine A   Medicine D

   Medicine B   Medicine E

   Medicine C
4. Choose a medicine label from those that your teacher has given to you.
5. What is the name of the medicine?
6. How often should someone your age take the medicine?
7. What is the medicine for?
8. When reading the medicine label, what warnings did you notice?

This book has words you may not have read before. Many of these words are science words. Some science words may be hard for you to read. You will find the science words in **bold print.** These words may appear two ways. The first way shows how the word is spelled. The second way shows how the word sounds. The list below shows the sounds each letter or group of letters makes.

Look at the word **energy** (EN ur jee). The second spelling shows the letters "ee." Find these letters in the list. The "ee" has the sound of "ea" in the word "leaf." Anytime you see "ee," you know what sound to say.

The capitalized syllable is the accented syllable.

a . . . back (BAK)
er . . . care, fair (KER, FER)
ay . . . day (DAY)
ah . . . father (FAHTH ur)
ar . . . car (KAR)
ow . . . flower, loud (FLOW ur, LOWD)
e . . . less (LES)
ee . . . leaf (LEEF)
ih . . . trip (TRIHP)
i (or i + *consonant* + e) . . . idea, life (i DEE uh, LIFE)
oh . . . go (GOH)
aw . . . soft (SAWFT)
or . . . orbit (OR but)
oy . . . coin (KOYN)

oo . . . foot (FOOT)
yoo . . . pure (PYOOR)
ew . . . food (FEWD)
yew . . . few (FYEW)
uh (or u + *consonant*) . . . comma, mother (KAHM uh, MUTH ur)
sh . . . shelf (SHELF)
ch . . . nature (NAY chur)
g . . . gift (GIHFT)
j . . . gem, edge (JEM, EJ)
ing . . . sing (SING)
zh . . . vision (VIHZH un)
k . . . cake (KAYK)
s . . . seed, cent (SEED, SENT)
z . . . zone, raise (ZOHN, RAYZ)

A

adaptation (ad ap TAY shun): anything that helps an animal live in its environment

alcohol (AL kuh hawl): a drug that slows down the way the body works

atmosphere (AT muh sfihr): all the air that surrounds Earth

atom (AT um): the smallest part of any kind of matter

B

behavior (bih HAY vyur): a living thing's response to something in its environment

C

caffeine (ka FEEN): a drug that speeds up the way the body works

cell (SEL): the smallest unit of living matter

chemical change: a change that takes place when a compound forms

circulatory (SUR kyuh luh tor ee) **system:** moves blood throughout your body

cirrus (SIHR us) **clouds:** thin clouds formed high in the atmosphere and made of ice

climate (KLI mut): the usual weather in an area year after year

clouds: formed from millions of water droplets, tiny pieces of ice, or both ice and water

community (kuh MYEW nut ee): a group of producers and consumers living together in one area

compound (KAHM pownd): a kind of matter formed from two or more elements

compound machine: a machine made of two or more simple machines

condensation (kahn den SAY shun): the change from a gas to a liquid

coniferous (kuh NIHF rus) **forest:** a forest habitat found in northern regions

consumer (kun SEW mur): a living thing that cannot make its own food

control (kun TROL): something that shows what happens when no changes are made in an experiment

core (KOR): the innermost part of Earth

crust (KRUST): the top layer of Earth

cumulus (KYEW myuh lus) **clouds:** large, puffy clouds

D

decomposer (dee kum POH zur): a living thing that breaks down dead plants and animals into simpler matter

desert (DEZ urt): a hot or cold habitat that has very little moisture

dew: water that condenses on objects near the ground

digestive (di JES tihv) **system:** changes the food you eat so that it can be used by your body

disease (dihz EEZ): an illness

drug: a substance that changes the way a body or mind works

E

element (EL uh munt): matter that is made of one kind of atom

endocrine (EN duh krun) **system:** is made of organs that make chemicals that control your body; some chemicals are important for growth

energy (EN ur jee): the ability to do work

erosion (ih ROH zhun): the movement of soil and rocks to new places

evaporation (ih vap uh RAY shun): the change from a liquid to a gas

F

feathers: strong, lightweight outer coverings of birds

food chain: the transfer of energy in a community

food web: all the feeding relationships in a community

force: a push or a pull

freshwater habitats: water habitat such as ponds, bogs, swamps, lakes, and rivers

friction (FRIHK shun): a force that slows down or stops moving objects

frost (FRAWST): ice that forms directly from water vapor

fur: a thick covering of soft hair on an animal's body

G

gas: matter that has no shape or size of its own

glacier (GLAY shur): a large mass of ice that moves

gram: a unit used to measure small amounts of mass

grassland: a habitat where most of the plants are grasses

gravity (GRAV ut ee): the pulling force between objects

groundwater: water that soaks into the ground

H

habitat (HAB uh tat): an area that supports the life needs of a plant or animal

hypothesis (hi PAHTH uh sus): an idea that has not been proved but is stated to be true for purposes of study and testing

I

igneous (IHG nee us) **rock:** rock that forms from cooled magma or lava

immunity (ihm YEW nut ee): the body's protection against certain diseases

inclined (IHN klind) **plane:** a simple machine with a sloped surface used to move objects

instinct (IHN stingt): a complex type of behavior an animal is born with

K

kilograms (Kee luh grams): units used to measure large amounts of mass; one kilogram equals 1000 grams

L

lava (LAHV uh): magma at Earth's surface

learned behavior: behavior that is caused by experience and can be changed

lever (LEV ur): a simple machine with an arm that rocks on a fulcrum

liquid (LIHK wud): matter that has a certain size but does not have its own shape

M

magma (MAG muh): hot liquid that forms inside Earth

mantle (MANT ul): the layer of Earth between the crust and the core

mass: how much there is of an object

matter: everything that takes up space and has mass

metamorphic (met uh MOR fihk) **rock:** rock that has been changed by heat and pressure

mineral (MIHN uh rul): solid matter found in nature but not made by plants or animals

mixture (MIHKS chur): a combination of two or more different types of matter in which each type of matter keeps its own properties

muscular system: made of muscle tissue and works with bones

N

nervous system: controls all your body actions; your brain, spinal cord, and nerves make up this system

nicotine (NIHK uh teen): a drug that speeds up the way the body works

O

organ: a group of tissues working together

organ system (SIHS tum): a group of organs working together

over-the-counter drug: a drug that can be bought without a doctor's prescription

P

perspiration (pur spuh RAY shun): liquid wastes that are released through sweat glands

physical change: a change in a physical property of matter

poisons (POY zunz): substances that are harmful to the body

polar region (POH lur • REE jun): an area of ice and snow near the poles

polar zones: areas on Earth where the temperatures are always cold

precipitation (prih sihp uh TAY shun): moisture that falls from the atmosphere

predator (PRED ut ur): an animal that hunts and eats other animals

prescription (prih SKRIHP shun) **drug:** a drug prepared after it is ordered by a doctor

prey (PRAY): animals eaten by predators

problem (PRAHB lum): a question for study

producer (pruh DEW sur): a living thing that makes its own food

property (PRAHP urt ee): is a characteristic of an object

pulley (POOL ee): a simple machine that has a rope wrapped around a wheel

R

rain forest: a hot forest habitat that receives large amounts of rainfall each year

reflex: the reaction of an animal to something in its environment

respiratory (RES pruh tor ee) **system:** makes the exchange of gases happen when you breathe

rock cycle (SI kul): the changing of rocks into different kinds of rocks

runoff: water that flows across the ground

S

saltwater habitat: a water habitat found in oceans

scales: small, thin plates that cover the skin of some animals

scavenger (SKAV un jur): an animal that feeds on dead plants and animals

scientific methods (si un TIHF ihk • METH udz): lists of steps that are used to study or explain something

screw: an inclined plane wrapped around a post

sedimentary (sed uh MENT uh ree) **rock:** rock made of sediments that are pressed together

sediments (SED uh munts:) small pieces of Earth material

shelter: a place or object that protects an animal

simple machine: a machine with few or no moving parts

skeletal (SKEL ut ul) **system:** gives your body shape and protects many organs

skin: the outer covering of an animal's body

solid (SAHL ud): matter that has a certain size and shape

stratus (STRAT us) **clouds:** clouds that cover the sky

T

temperate (TEM prut) **forest:** a forest habitat with four seasons—spring, summer, autumn, and winter

temperate zones: areas on Earth where the weather changes during four seasons of the year

tissue (TIHSH ewz): a group of cells working together

tropics: area on Earth where the temperatures are always hot

tundra (TUN druh): a cold, dry habitat with a layer of soil that is frozen

U

urethra (yoo REE thruh): releases urine from your body

urinary (YOOR uh ner ee) **system:** is made up of organs that remove liquid wastes from your body

urine (YOOR un): the wastes and water removed from your body

V

vaccine (vak SEEN): dead or weakened germs that give immunity to a disease

variables (VER ee uh bulz): things that change in an experiment

W

water cycle (SI kul): the continuous movement of water through the different stages of evaporation, condensation, precipitation, and storage

water vapor (VAY pur): water as a gas

weathering: the breaking down or wearing away of rock

wedge (WEJ): a simple machine made of two inclined planes

wheel and axle (AK sul): a simple machine with a wheel that turns a post

wildlife conservation (kahn sur VAY shun): the protection of habitats and living things

work: what is done when a force moves an object

Index

Experiments, 10–22; controls of, 14; variables of, 14–15; *act.,* 9, 22

F

Feathers, 251–252; *illus.,* 251

Feet, 254–255

Flooding, 175

Fog, 155

Food, consumers, 198–211; in digestive system, 294; as energy, 80, 194, 207, 211, 295; groups of, 307–308; healthful, 306–310, 313; importance of, 194; producers, 195–198, 202, 206–209, 240; *act.,* 201, 309; *illus.,* 194–196, 198, 208, 212, 306–308; *table,* 307, 309

Food chains, 208–212, 240; *act.,* 209

Food webs, 210–212; *illus.,* 210

Forces, 70–82; friction, 75–77, 83–84; gravity, 74; and inclined planes, 94–95; and levers, 90–93; and pulleys, 99–101; and work, 78–80; *act.,* 73, 77; *illus.,* 70–72, 91

Forests, 230–233; coniferous, 230–231; rain, 232–233; temperate, 231–232; *illus.,* 230–233

Freshwater habitats, 234; *illus.,* 234

Friction, 75–77, 83–84; *act.,* 76–77; *illus.,* 75

Frost, 152

Fuels, 80–82; *illus.,* 80–81

Fulcrums, 90–92; *illus.,* 91

Fur, 252; *illus.,* 252

G

Gases, 34, 38, 42–43; carbon dioxide, 195, 286, 295–296; changing, 51, 59–60, 151–152; oxygen, 194, 295–296; *illus.,* 34, 42

Germs, 310–314

Glaciers, 136; and erosion, 142

Glands, 300; sweat, 298

Grams, 31–32

Grasslands, 228–229; *illus.,* 228–229

Gravity, 74; and groundwater, 176; and runoff, 174

Groundwater, 176, 183; *act.,* 179; *illus.,* 176

H

Habitats, 218–240; deserts, 227–229; forests, 230–233;

373

Photo Credits

Cover: Leonard Nolt

iv, Studiohio; **v,** (t) Steve Lissau, (b) Latent Image; **viii,** Studiohio; **x,** (t) Studiohio, (b) Mark Burnett/Merrill photo; **xi,** Stephen Dalton/Photo Researchers; **xii,** Michael Tamborrino/FPG; **xiii,** NASA; **xiv,** Doug Martin; **xv,** Richard Hutchings/Photo Researchers; **xvi,** (tl) The Stock Market/Michael D. Newler 1982, (cr) Doug Martin 1990, (bl) Studiohio; **1** (tr) Animals Animals/C.C. Lockwood, (cl) Studiohio, (cr) The Bettmann Archive; **2, 4,** Kenji Kerins; **5,** Diane Graham-Henry and Kathleen Culbert-Aguilar; **6, 7, 8,** Doug Martin; **9,** Elaine Shay; **10, 13,** Mary Lou Uttermohlen; **16,** Doug Martin; **17,** Studiohio; **18,** Brent Turner/BLT Productions; **19,** Doug Martin; **20,** Studiohio; **26,** Bob Daemmrich; **27,** Diane Graham-Henry and Kathleen Culbert-Aguilar; **28,** Tim Courlas; **29, 30, 31,** Studiohio; **32—33,** Latent Image; **33,** Cobalt Productions; **34,** (t) Studiohio, (l) Tom McGuire, (r) The Stock Market/Barry Seidman; **35,** (t) Jack Sekowski, (b) Latent Image; **36,** (t) Latent Image, (c) Carolina Biological Supply, (b) file photo; **37, 39,** Latent Image; **40,** Jack Sekowski; **41,** Latent Image; **42–43,** Steve Lissau; **42,** David M. Dennis; **43,** Latent Image; **44,** Cobalt Productions; **47,** Steve Lissau; **48,** Paul Chauncey/The Stock Market; **49,** Diane Graham-Henry and Kathleen Culbert-Aguilar; **51, 52,** Milepost Corp.; **53,** Jeff Clark; **54,** Tim Courlas; **56,** Ted Rice; **58,** Mary Lou Uttermohlen; **59,** Jack Sekowski; **60,** Aaron Haupt/Merrill photo; **61,** Cobalt Productions; **62,** (l) Studiohio, (r) Doug Martin; **63,** Milepost Corp.; **64,** Tom McGuire; **65,** Royce Bair/Stock Solution/High Pressure Press at facility of Sii Megadiamond in Provo, UT; **68,** Kenji Kerins; **69,** Diane Graham-Henry and Kathleen Culbert-Aguilar; **70,** Bob Daemmrich; **72, 73,** Milepost Corp.; **74, 75,** Doug Martin; **76,** Jack Sekowski; **78–79,** Bob Daemmrich; **80,** (l) Milepost Corp., (r) Pictures Unlimited; **81,** (l) Morgan Photos, (r) Milepost Corp.; **82, 83,** Milepost Corp.; **84,** Ron Johnson; **86,** Kenji Kerins; **87,** Bob Daemmrich; **90,** Studiohio; **92,** Gerard Photography; **95,** (t, b) Tim Courlas, (c) Aaron Haupt/Merrill photo; **96,** Studiohio; **97,** Cobalt Productions; **98,** Doug Martin; **99,** (l) Studiohio, (r) Bob Daemmrich; **100,** Doug Martin; **101,** Aaron Haupt/Merrill photo; **102,** Studiohio; **104,** (t) Edna Douthat, (b) William D. Popejoy; **105,** Doug Martin; **108–109,** Aaron Haupt/Merrill photo; **110,** Kenji Kerins; **112,** Walter Frerck/Odessey Productions; **114,** (t) Doug Martin, (b) Daniel A. Erickson; **115,** (l) Ted Rice, (tr) Linda Young, (cr, br) University of Houston; **118,** Daniel A. Erickson; **119,** Studiohio; **120–121,** Photri; **122–123,** David L. Perry; **123,** (t) file photo, (b) Earth Scenes © Breck P. Kent; **124,** (l) University of Houston, (r) Craig Kramer; **125,** Studiohio; **127,** (l) Craig Kramer, (c) Linda Young, (r) University of Houston; **128,** Cobalt Productions; **129,** Doug Martin; **131,** Studiohio; **132,** Jim Brown/The Stock Market; **133,** Ron Bishop/Stock Boston; **135,** (l) Roger K. Burnard, (r) Studiohio; **136,** (t) file photo, (b) Roger K. Burnard; **137,** (l) Barry L. Runk from Grant Heilman, (r) Elaine Shay; **138,** (l) Tim Courlas, (r) Jim Strawser from Grant Heilman; **141,** Studiohio; **142,** Michael Collier; **143,** Cobalt Productions; **144,** Philip LaRocco; **146,** Ellis Herwig/Stock Boston; **148, 149,** Gerard Photography; **151,** Latent Image; **152,** Debbie Dean; **153,** Cobalt Productions; **154,** Earth Scenes/Richard Kolar; **155,** (l) John D. Pearce, (r) file photo; **156,** Earth Scenes/Breck P. Kent; **158,** Dave Watts/Tom Stack & Associates; **159,** (l) David M. Dennis, (tr) Mark Burnett/Merrill photo, (br) Larry Lefever from Grant Heilman; **161,** Lawrence Migdale; **162,** (tl) Bob Daemmrich/Image Works, (bl) Steve Lissau, (r) Ed Shay; **163,** Tony Stone Worldwide; **165,** Mark Miller/Stock Imagery; **166,** Jeff Gnass/The Stock Market; **167,** Diane Graham-Henry and Kathleen Culbert-Aguilar; **168–169,** Aaron Haupt/Merrill photo; **168,** (l) Rich Brommer, (r) Aaron Haupt/Merrill photo; **169,** (t) Aaron Haupt/Merrill photo, (b) Gerard Photography; **170,** Mark Burnett/Merrill photo; **172,** Rick Kocks; **173,** Cobalt Productions; **174,** Earth Scenes/Michael P. Gadomski; **175,** Grand Heilman Photography; **177,** (tl) Tim Courlas, (bl) Steve Lissau, (r) Doug Martin; **178,** Steve Lissau; **179,** Cobalt Productions; **180,** Photri; **181,** Frank S. Balthis; **182,** Ken Graham/Bruce Coleman, Inc.; **183,** David M. Dennis; **184,** file photo; **186,** Pictures Unlimited; **188–189,** Aaron Haupt/Merrill photo; **190,** Animals Ani-